Stained No More

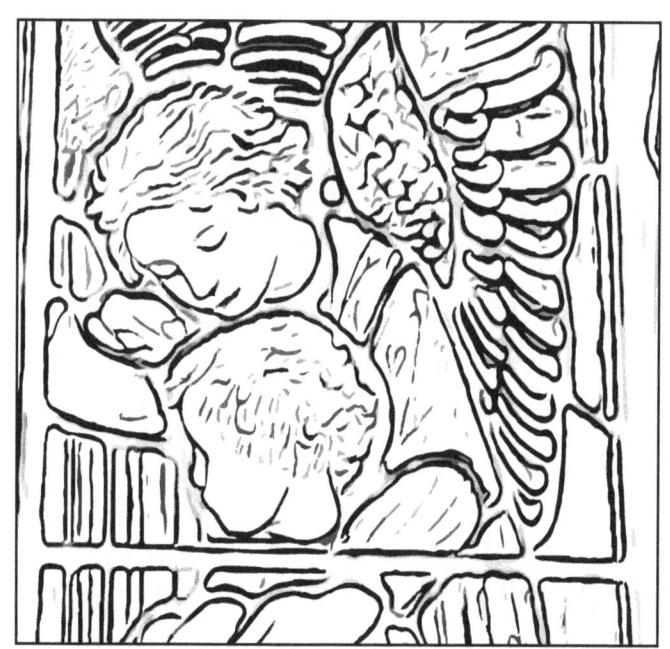

An Adult Christian Coloring Book
of Beautiful Church Windows

Brian C. Newman

Published by GREAT COLORADO BOOKS in 2015
First Edition; First Printing

Illustrations and design © 2015 Brian C. Newman

Cover photo used under license from Adobe Stock.

Fly page image is a derivative of "Veronica Whall window in Keswick church" by jmc4 Church explorer, used under CC BY by Brian C. Newman.

www.GreatColoradoBooks.com
www.StainedNoMore.com

Scripture quotations are taken from the Open English Bible, www.OpenEnglishBible.org.

ISBN 978-1517783761

Introduction

I admit it. As a young boy sitting in a small Baptist church on Sunday, I rarely listened to the preacher's sermon. Instead, I twitched, fidgeted, and made creative figurines with the foil of my Juicy Fruit gum wrapper. I also marveled at the stained glass windows in my church's windows, dedicated to many couples who had long since passed. There were intricate designs and different colors meshed together that reflected a church of faith in God, Jesus Christ, and the Holy Spirit. It definitely took a master craftsman to create something so beautiful.

In this coloring book designed for the adult Christian, I have searched my local community and the world (via the Internet) for some of the most beautiful, colorful, and intricate stained glass windows among houses of worship. I have left the patterns in place while removing the colors, giving you the opportunity to create your own masterpiece to express your faith. In some cases, I have transformed the designs further to create something special for meditative focus and clarity.

This coloring book is designed for the adult Christian, one who has experienced both the deep sorrows and the uplifting joys of this life. The stories, grace, and hope reflected in these designs will help you remember and rely on the promises that God has for each of us and the faith that we hold dear.

Instructions

- First, ensure you have coloring pencils. I recommend US Art Supply 50 Piece Artist Grade High Quality Colored Pencil Set, available from Amazon.com. You can find a link at www.StainedNoMore.com.
- Second, put on Christian music. I recommend your local WAY-FM station, The Message on Sirius XM, or your favorite CD or playlist.
- Third, choose a page to color, at random or in order -- It is totally up to you!
- Finally, meditate on God's word, the creativity that inspired these beautiful windows and the color that you and God bring forth together, in this time together.

If you have any feedback, comments, or suggestions are welcome, please contact me at GreatColoradoBooks@gmail.com or visit my web site at www.StainedNoMore.com.

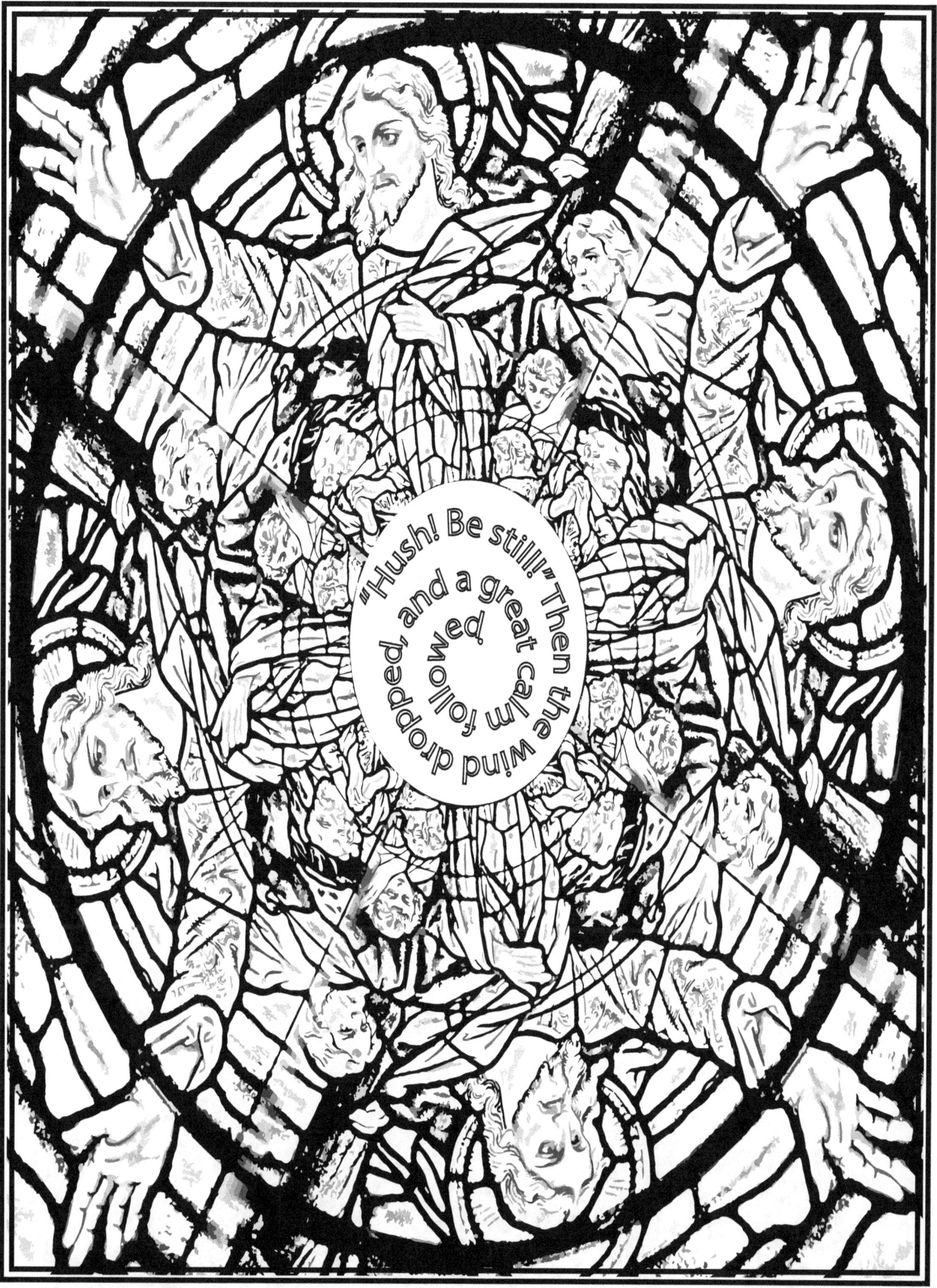

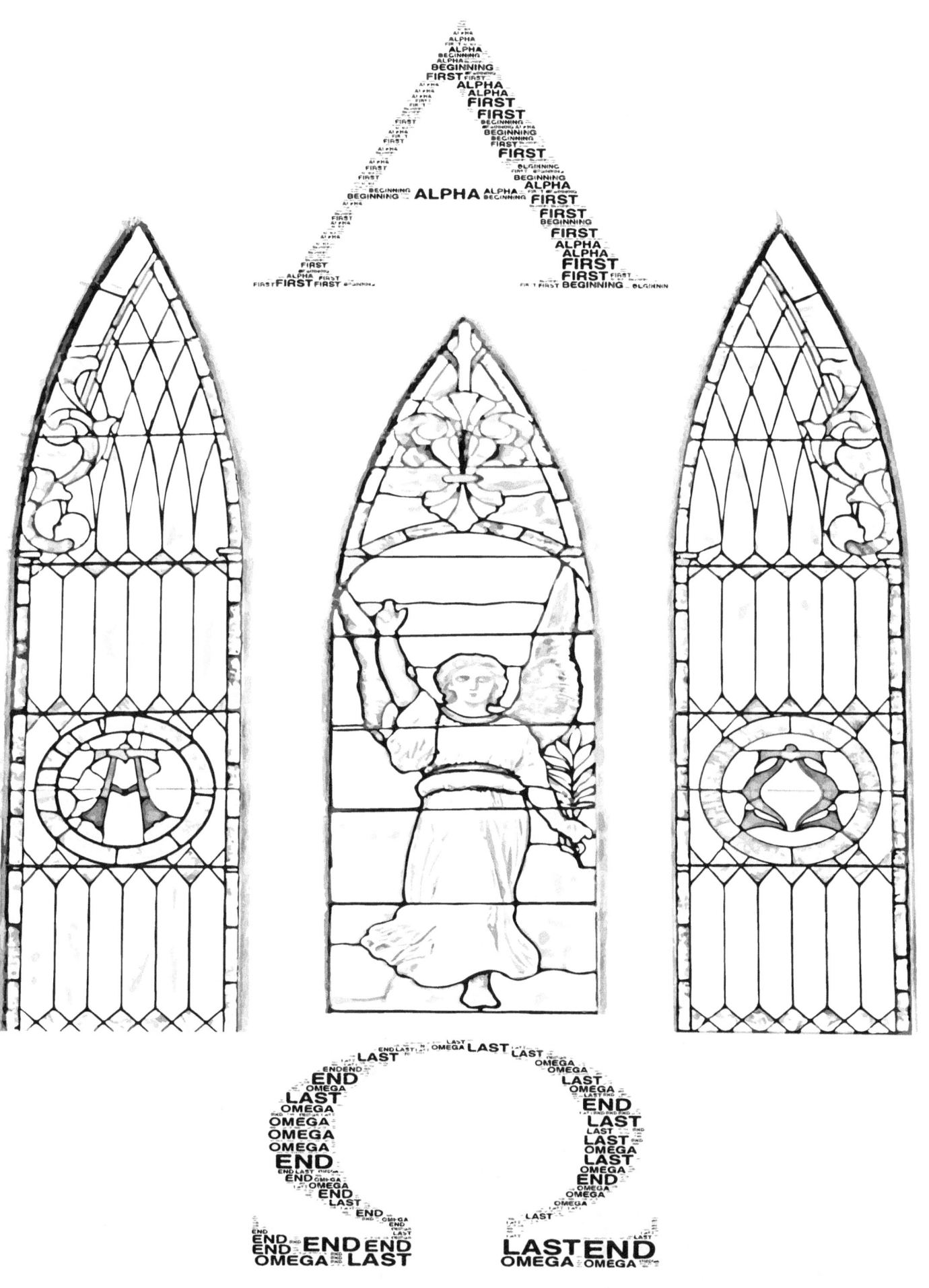

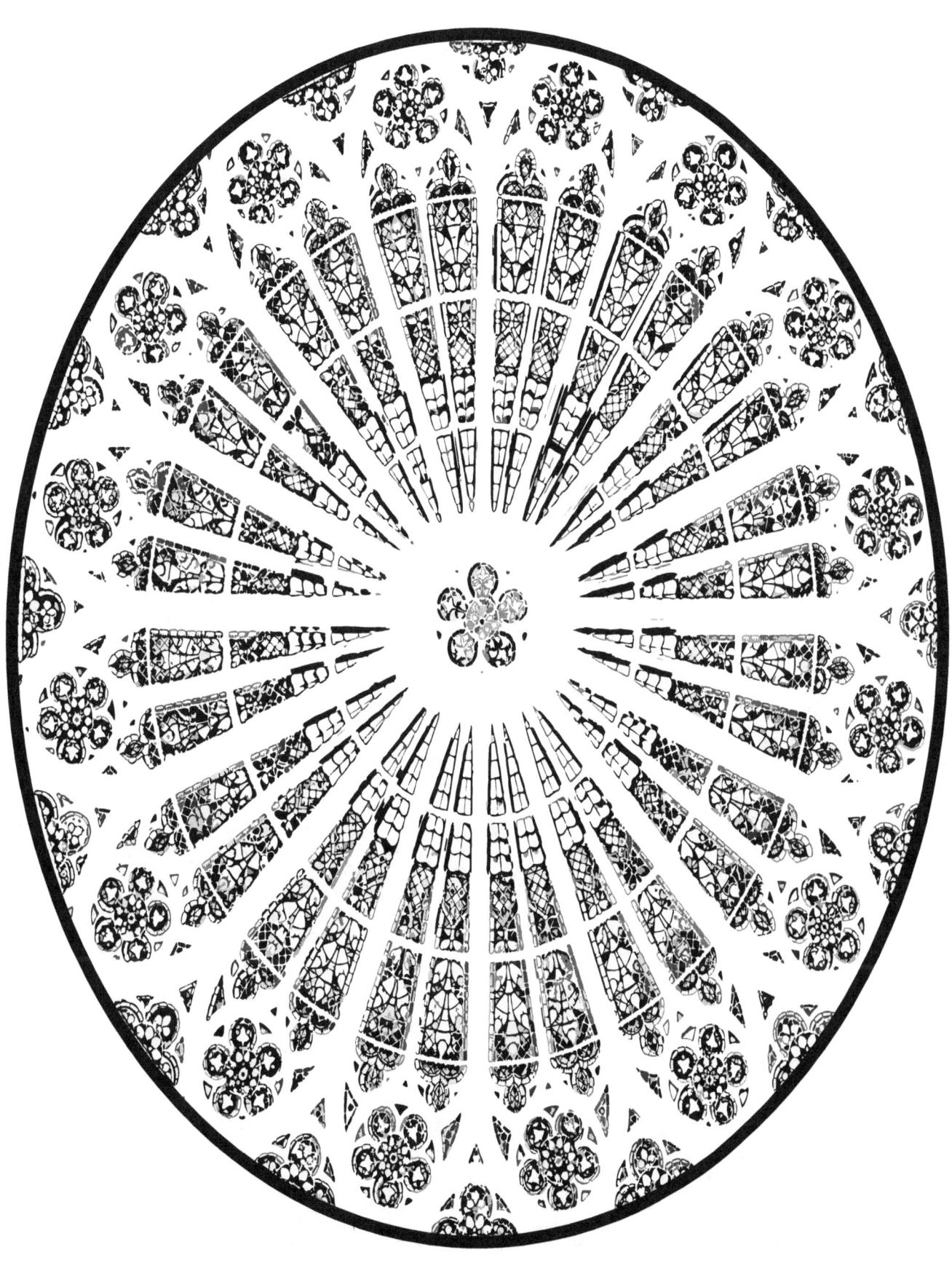

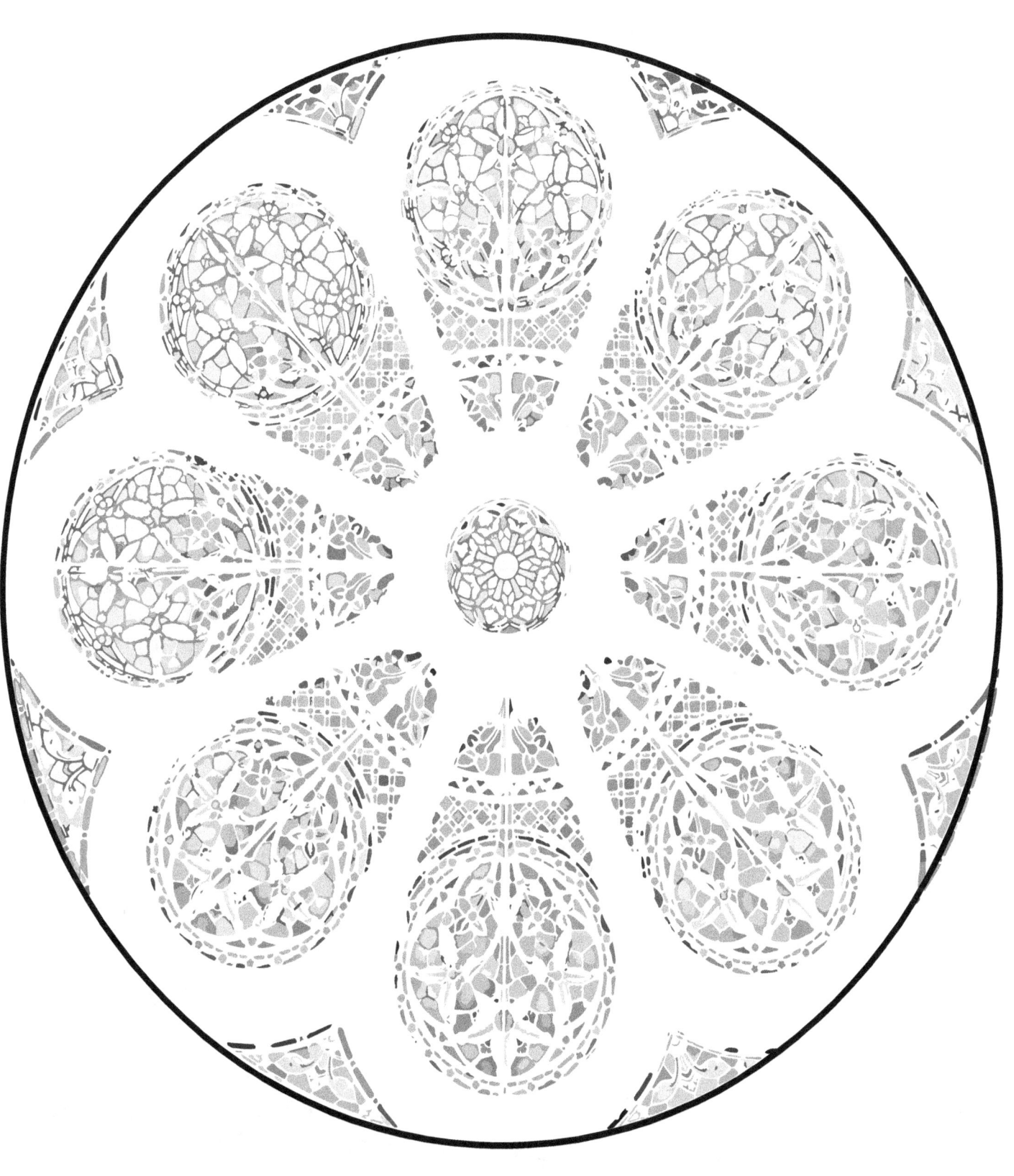

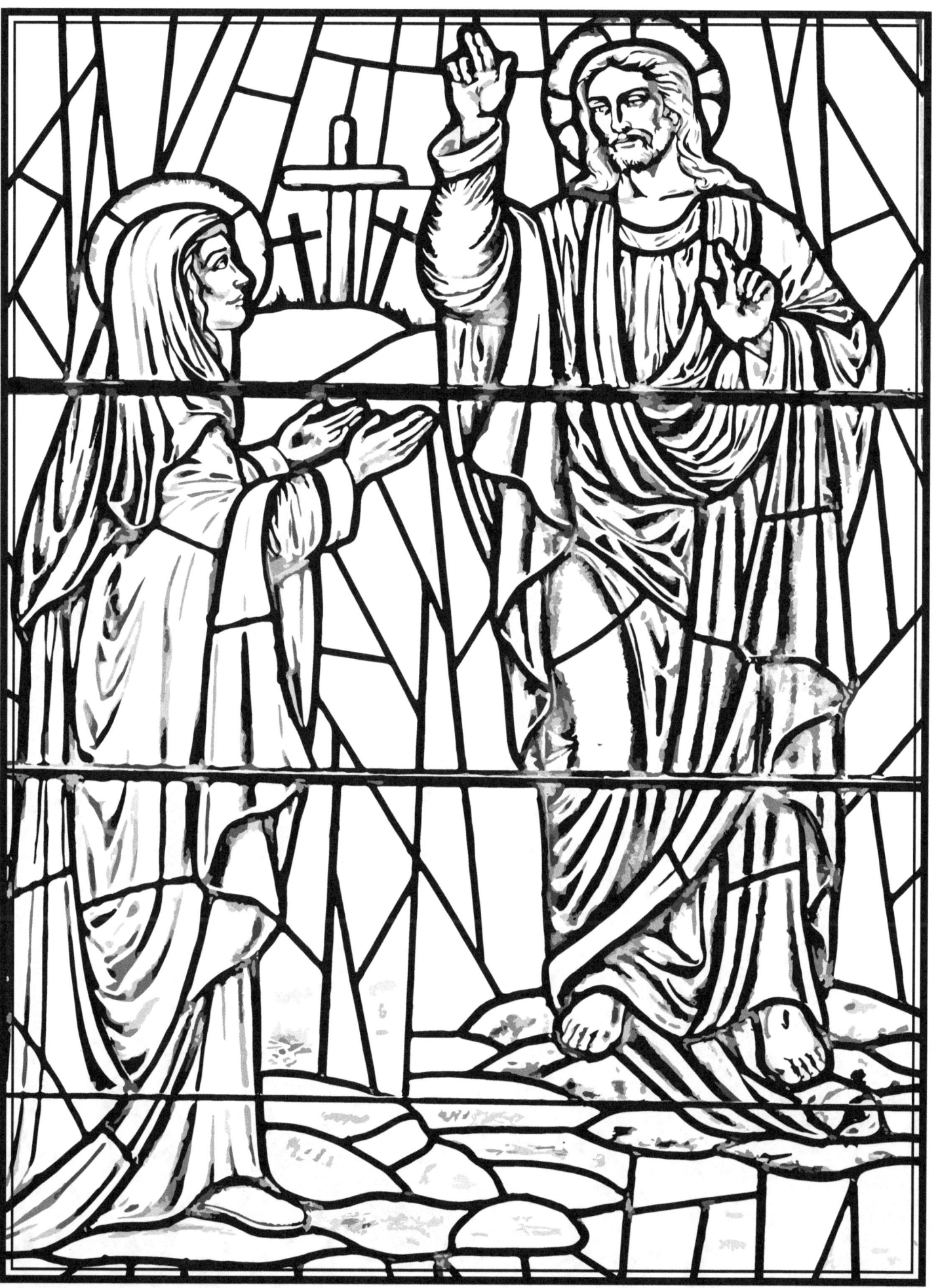

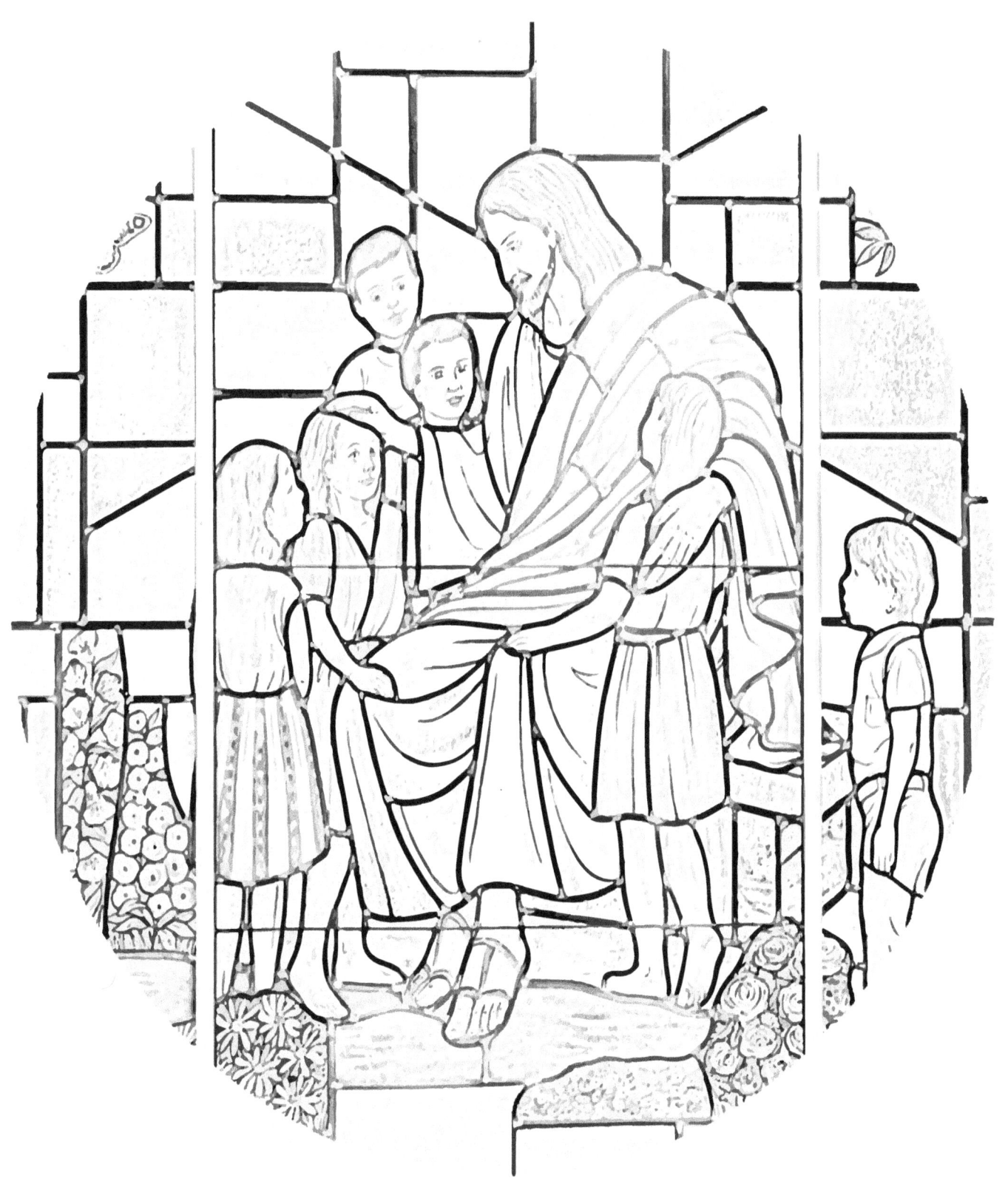

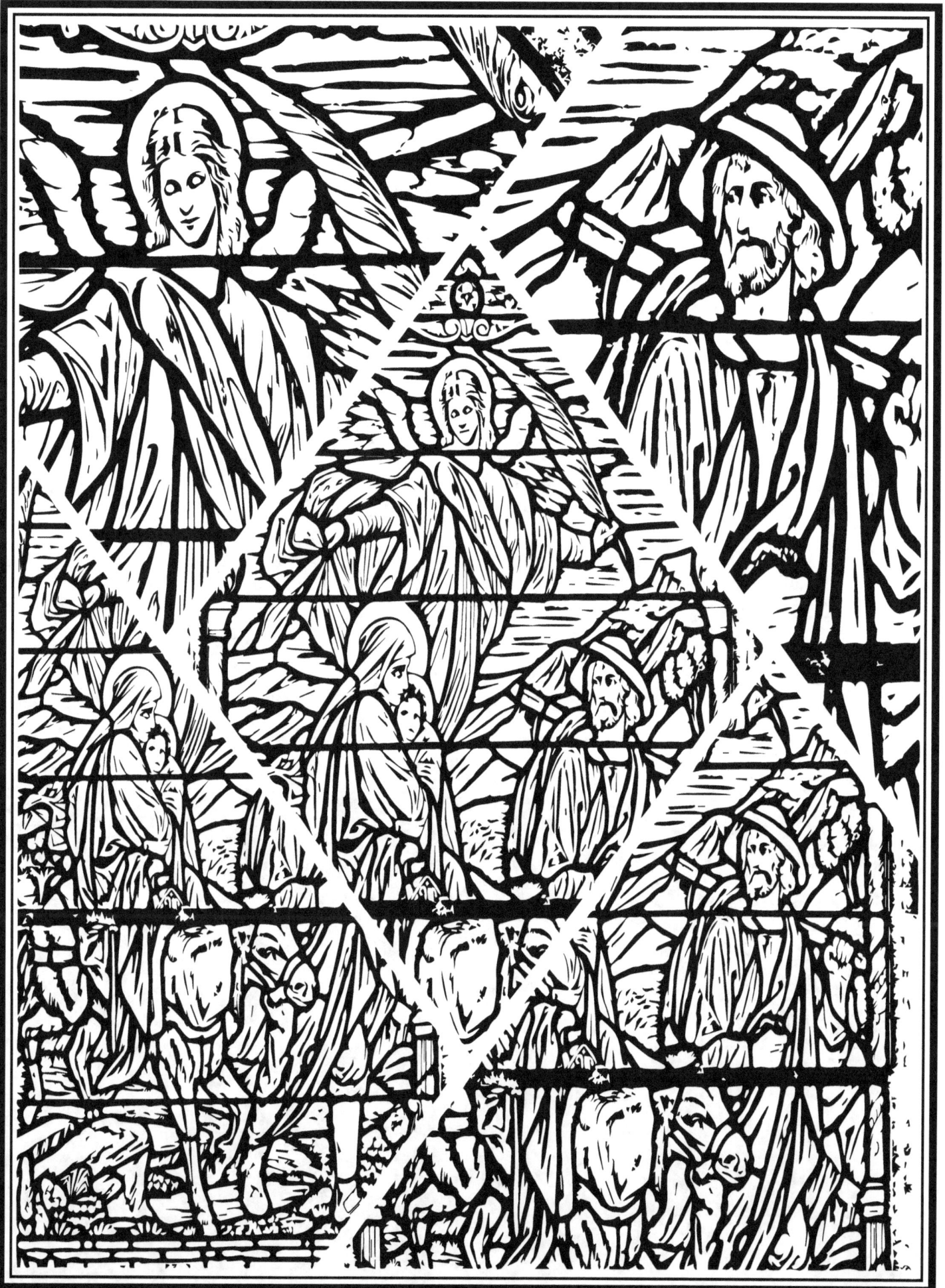

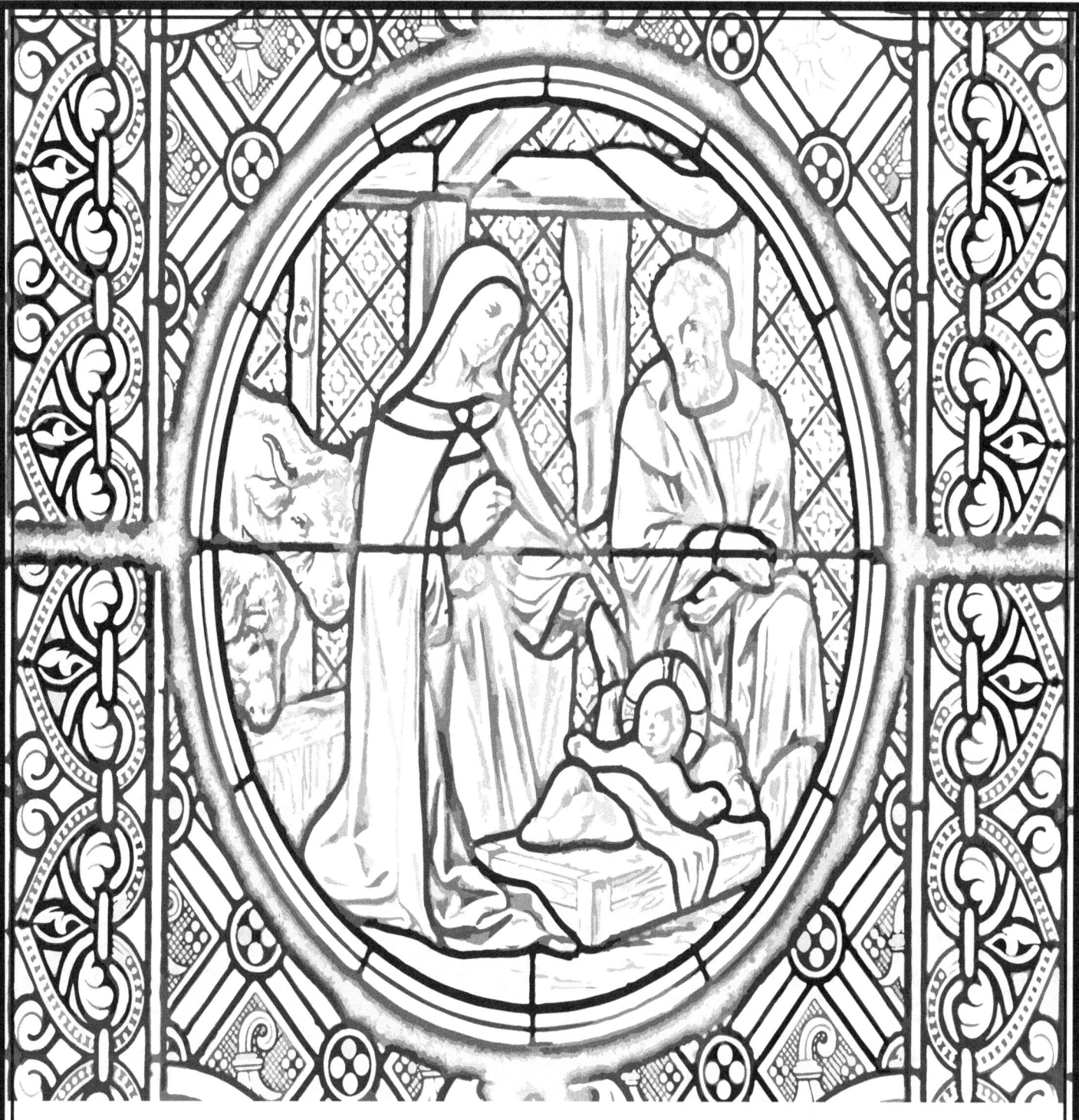

"Have no fear," the angel said. "For I bring you good news of a great joy in store for all the nation. This day there has been born to you, in the town of David, a Savior, who is Christ and Lord. And this will be the sign for you. You will find the infant swathed, and lying in a manger." Matthew 2: 10-12 OEB

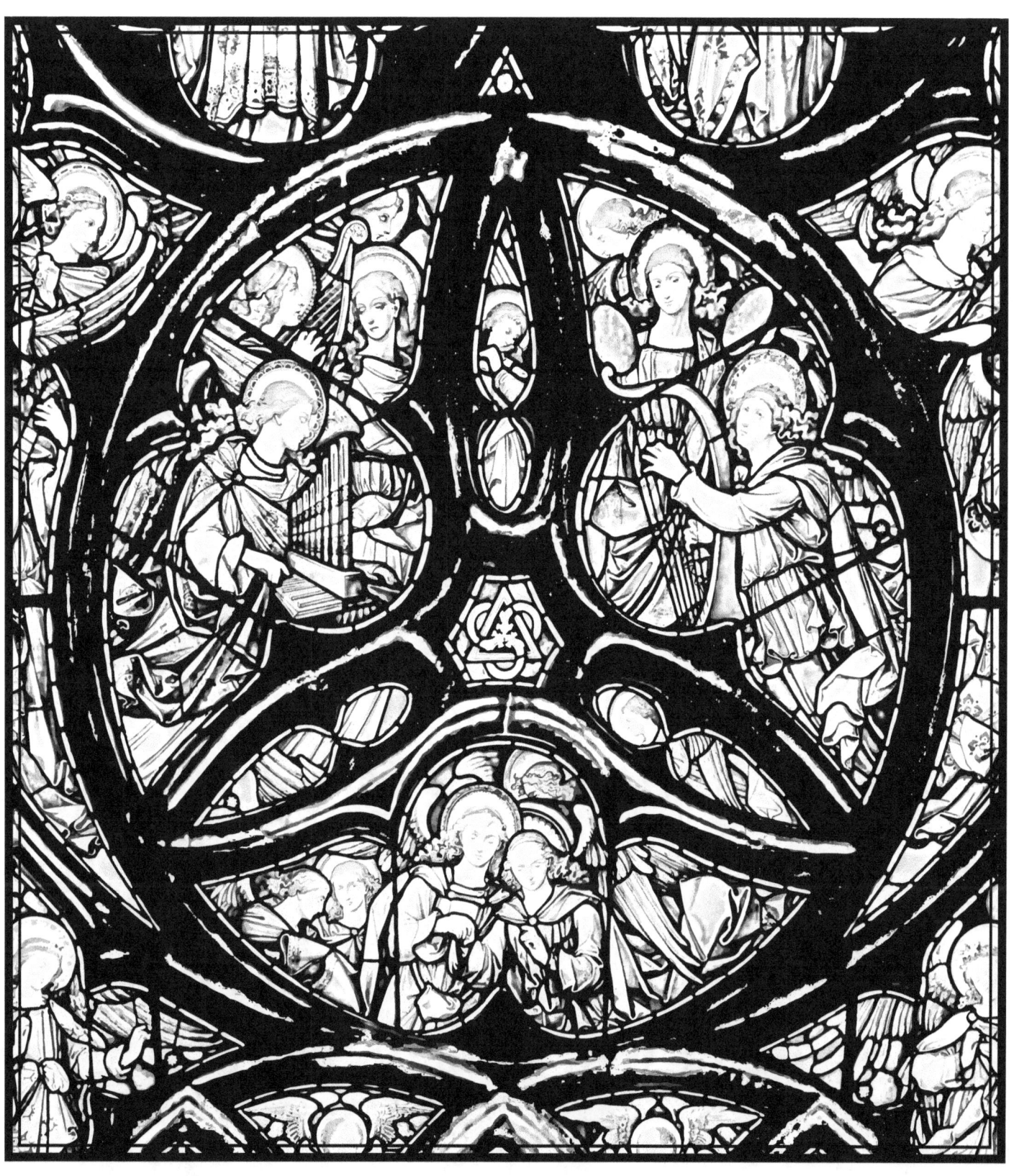

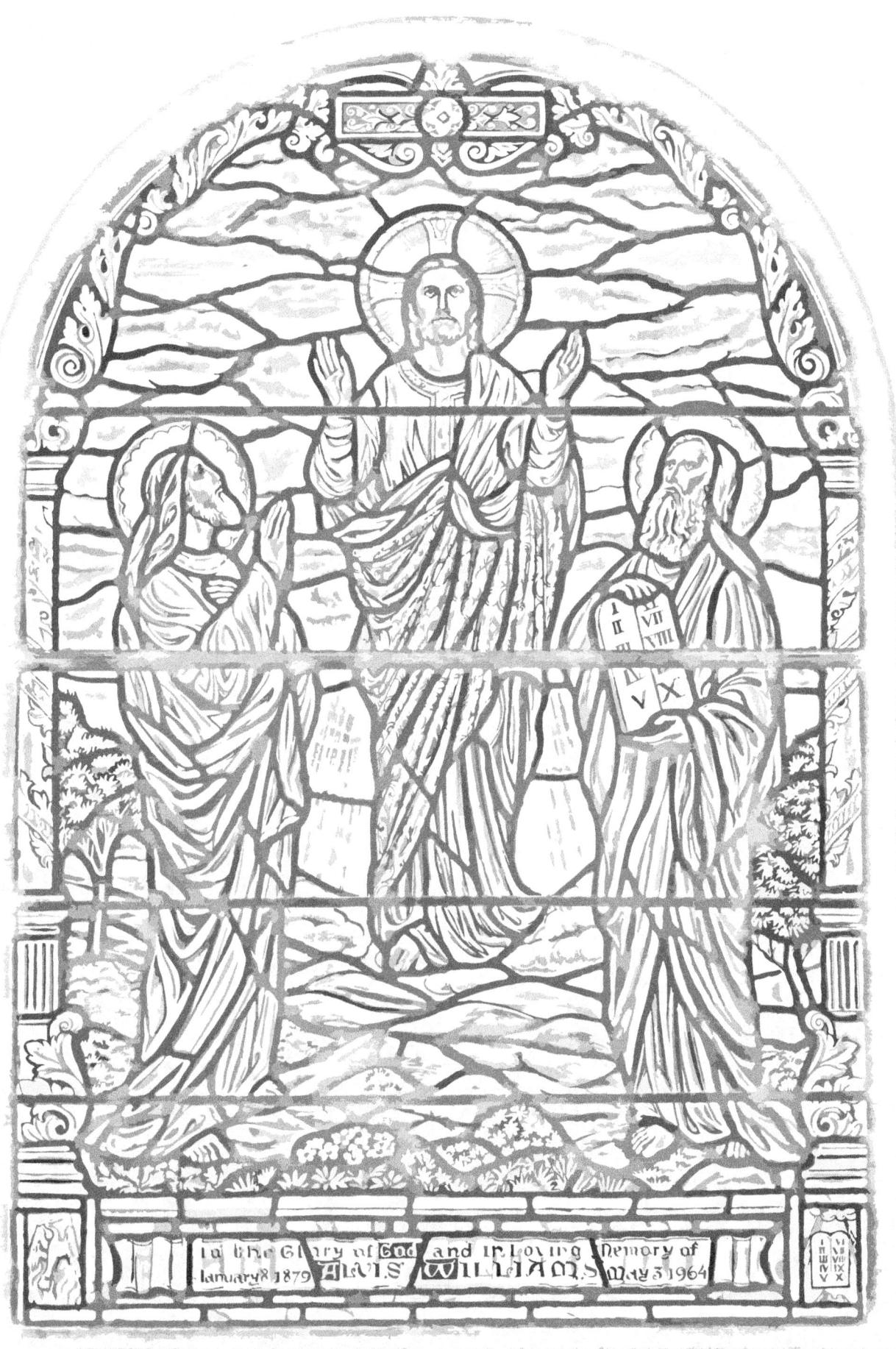

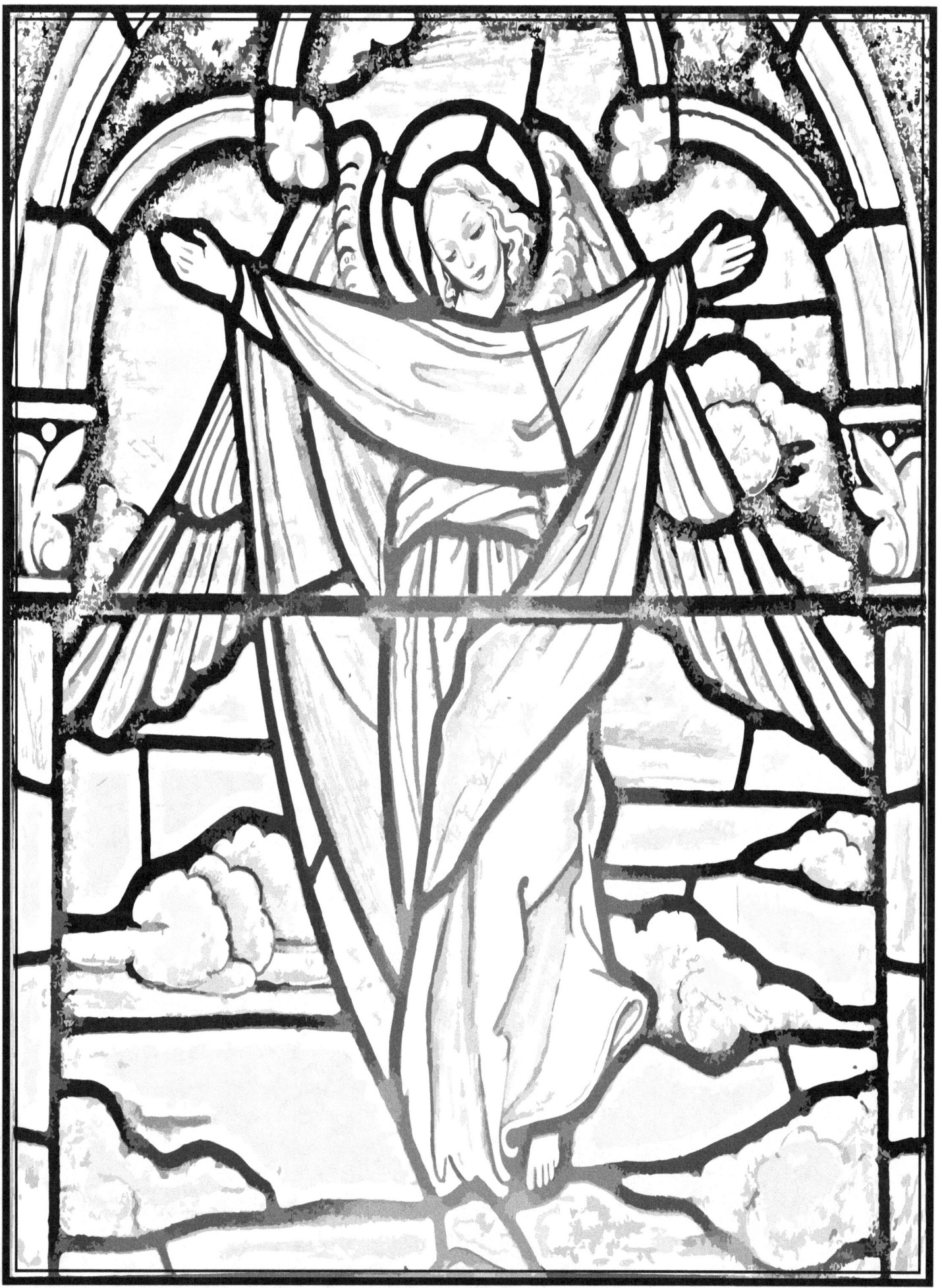

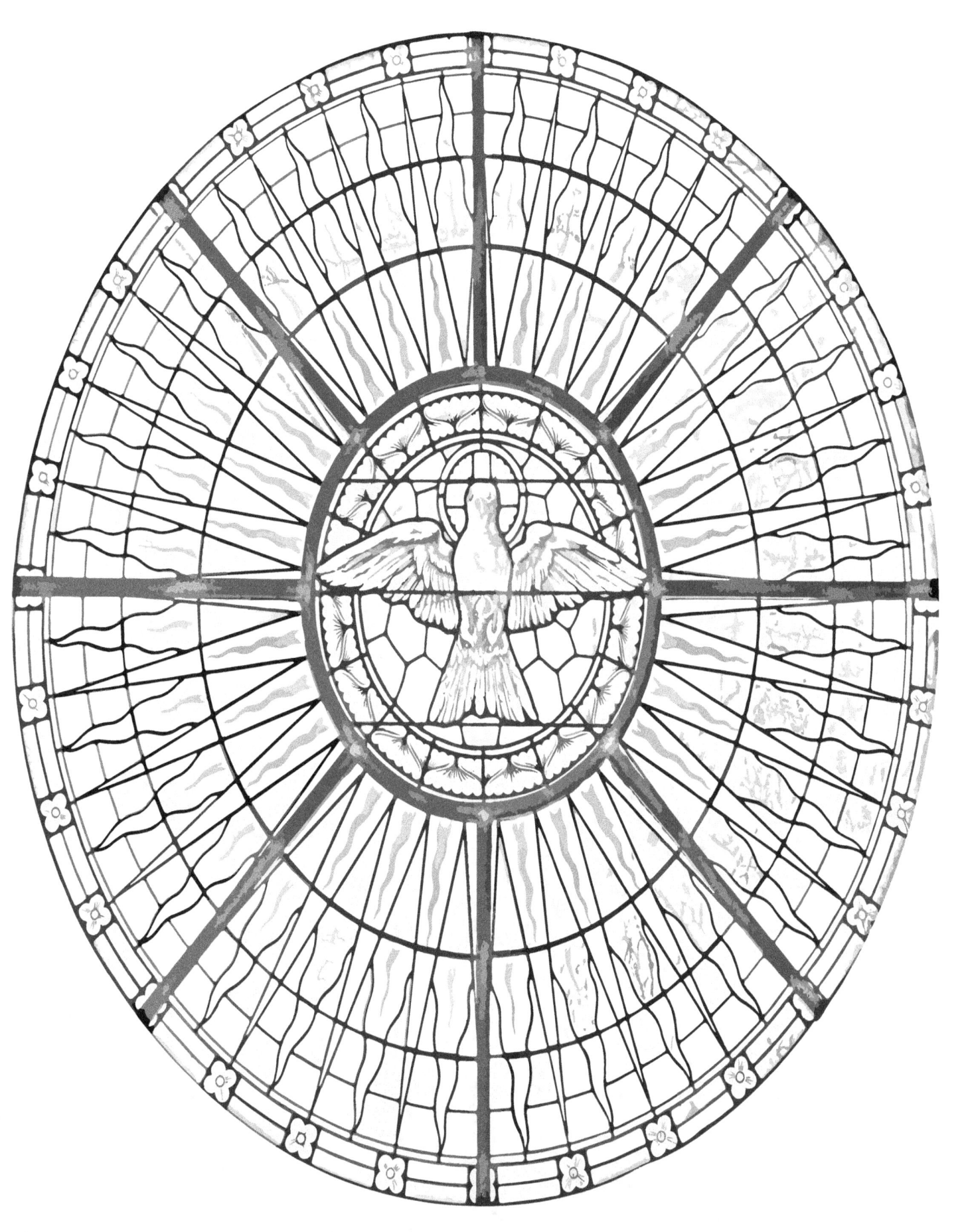

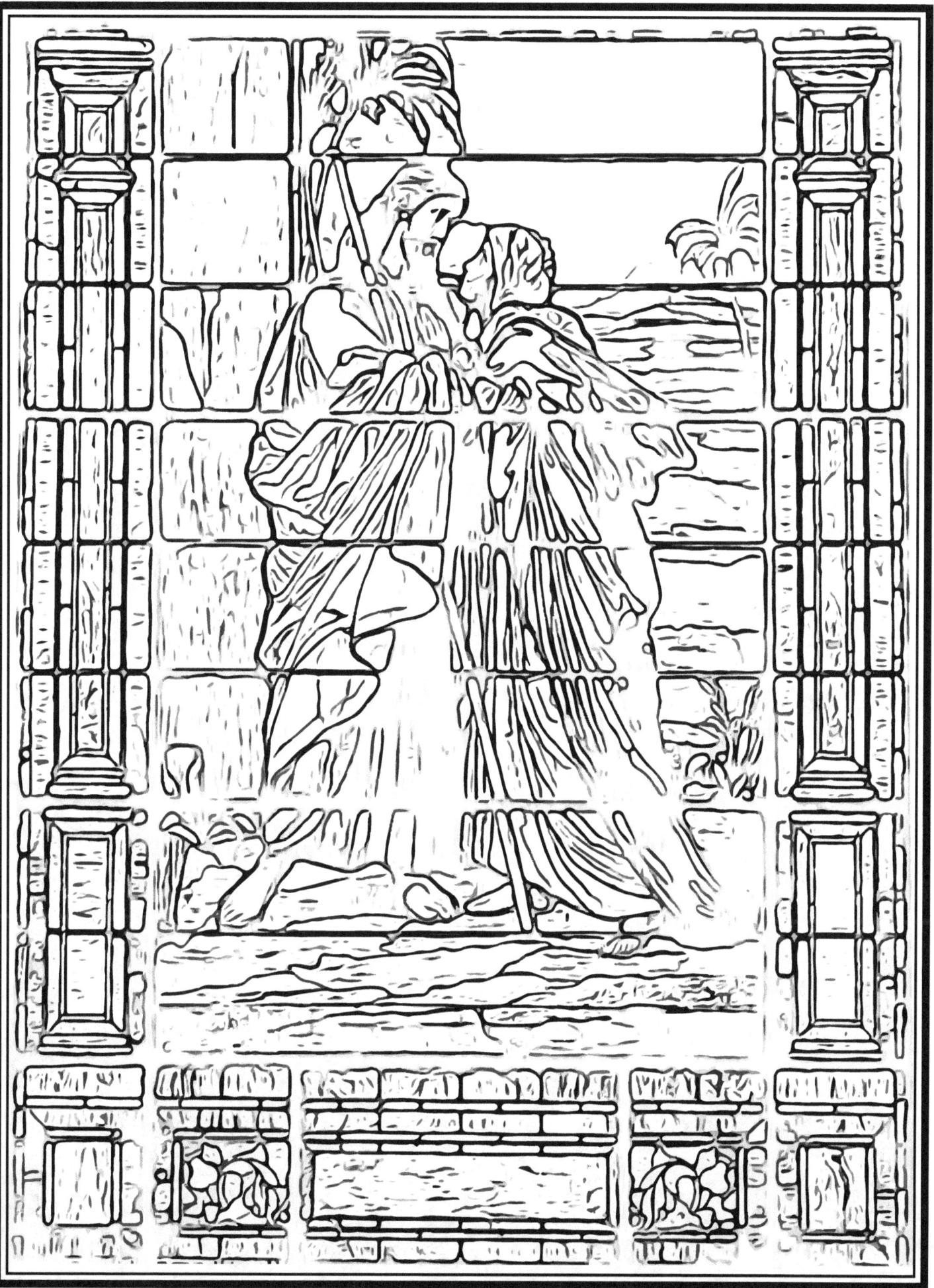

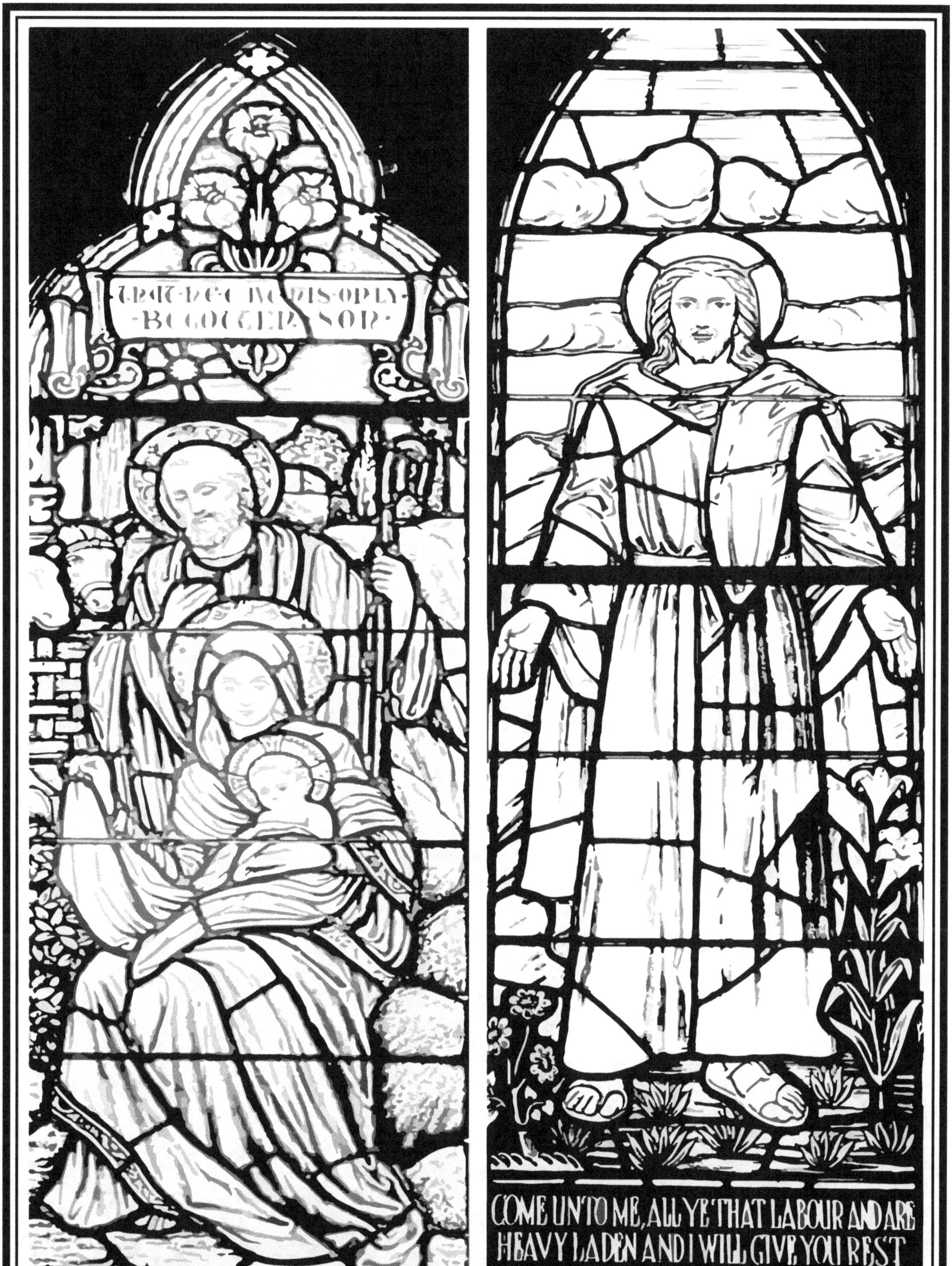

THAT THOU WAST OPLY
BEGOTTEN SON

COME UNTO ME, ALL YE THAT LABOUR AND ARE
HEAVY LADEN AND I WILL GIVE YOU REST

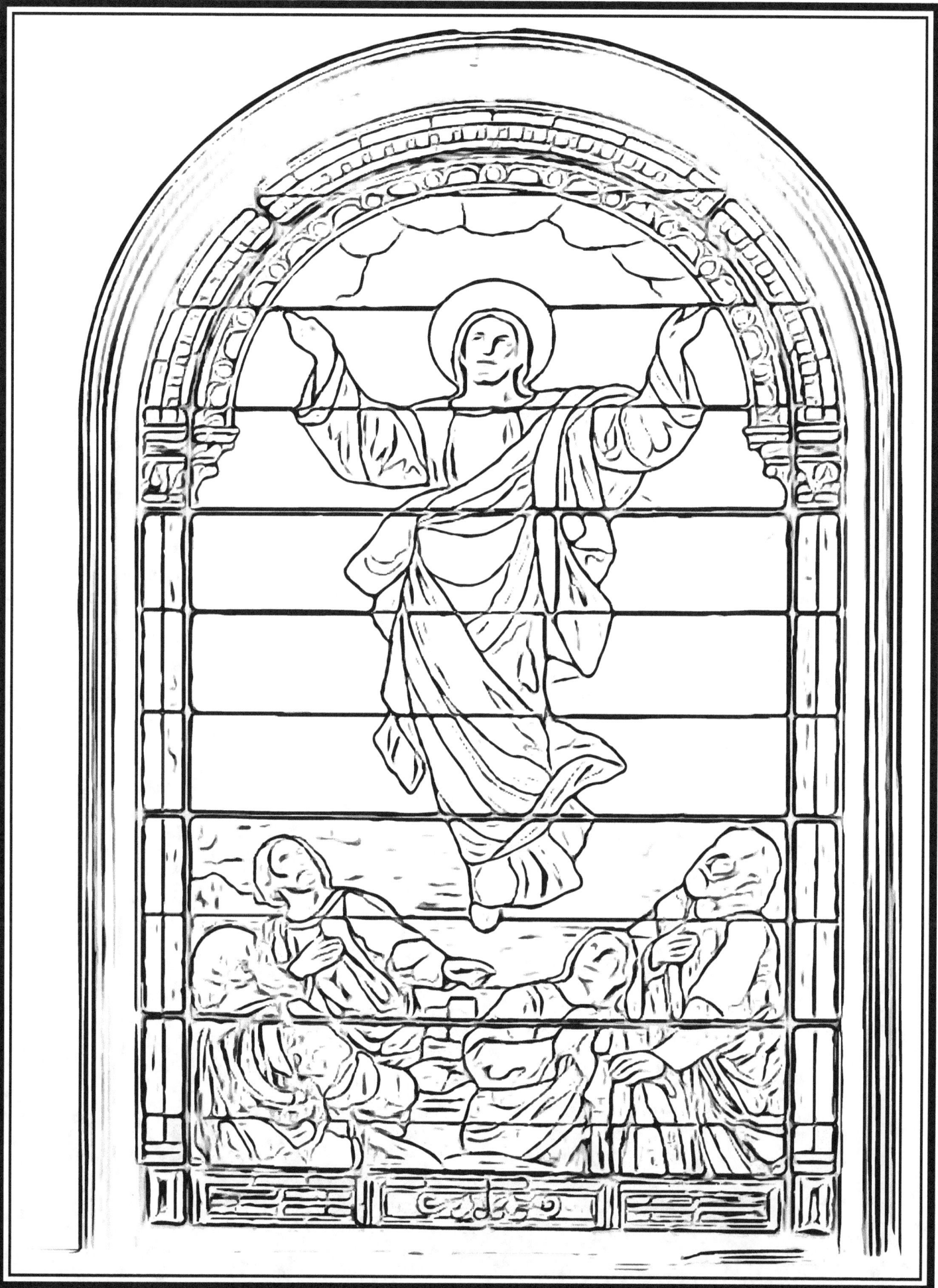

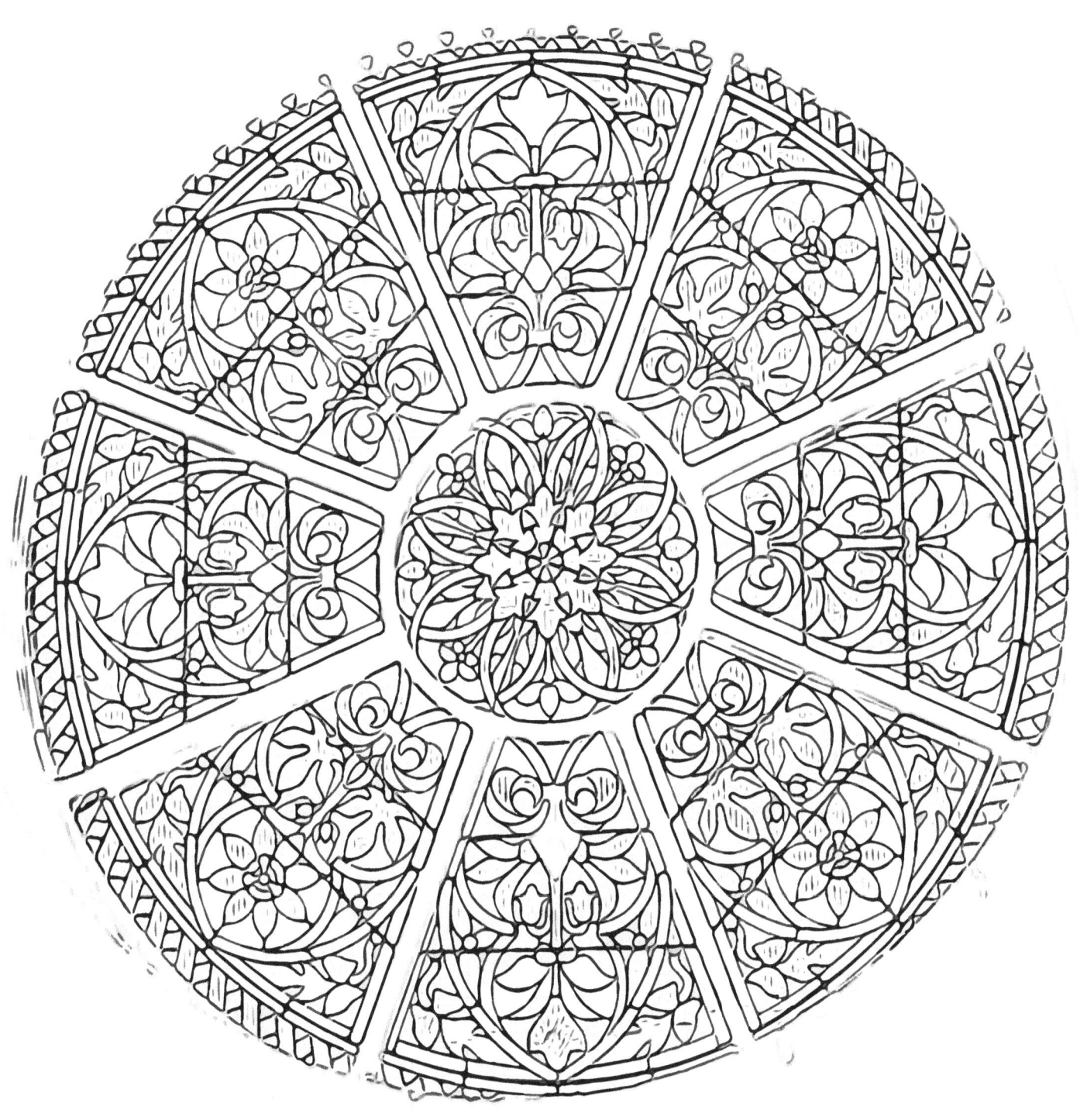

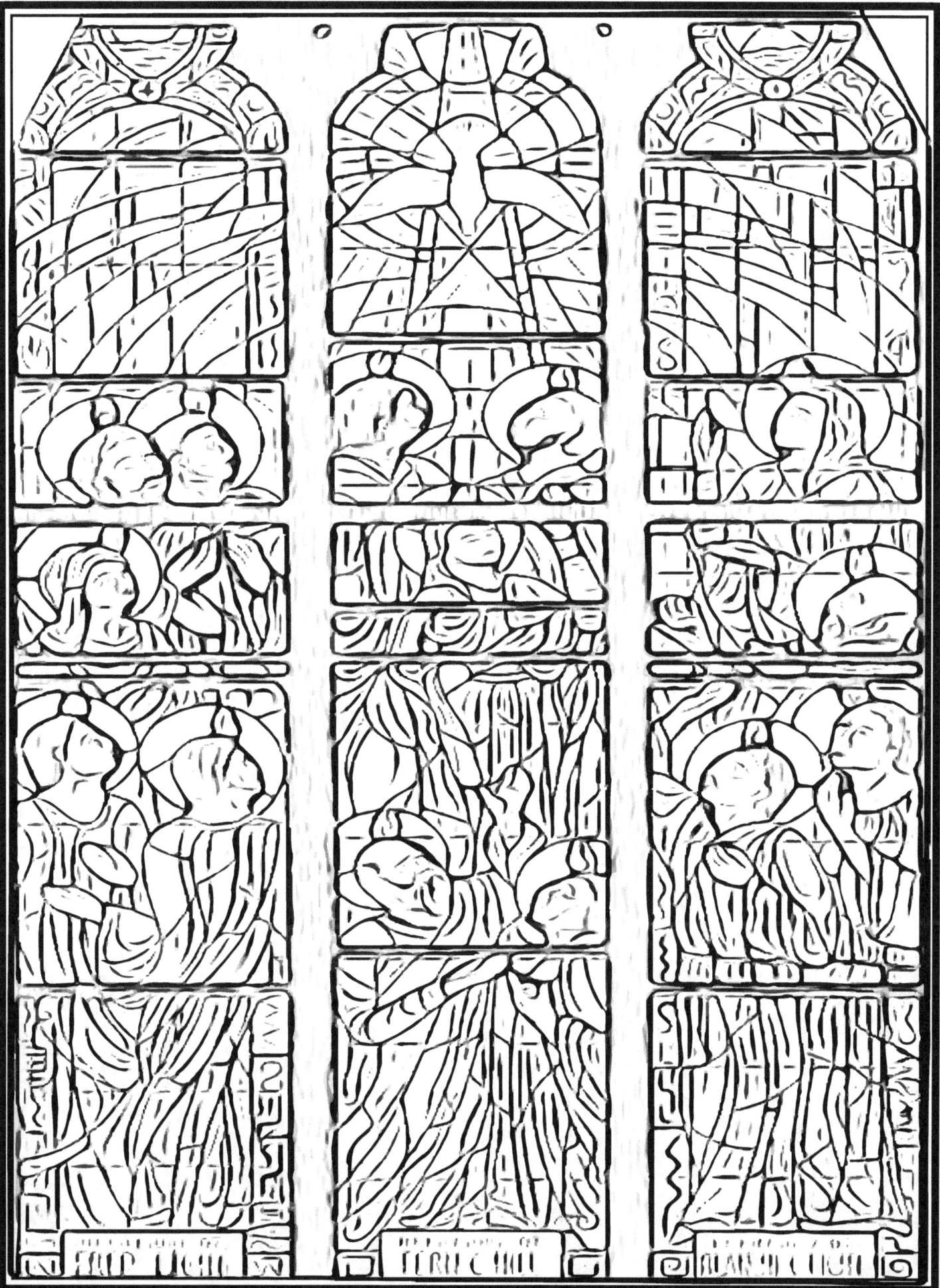

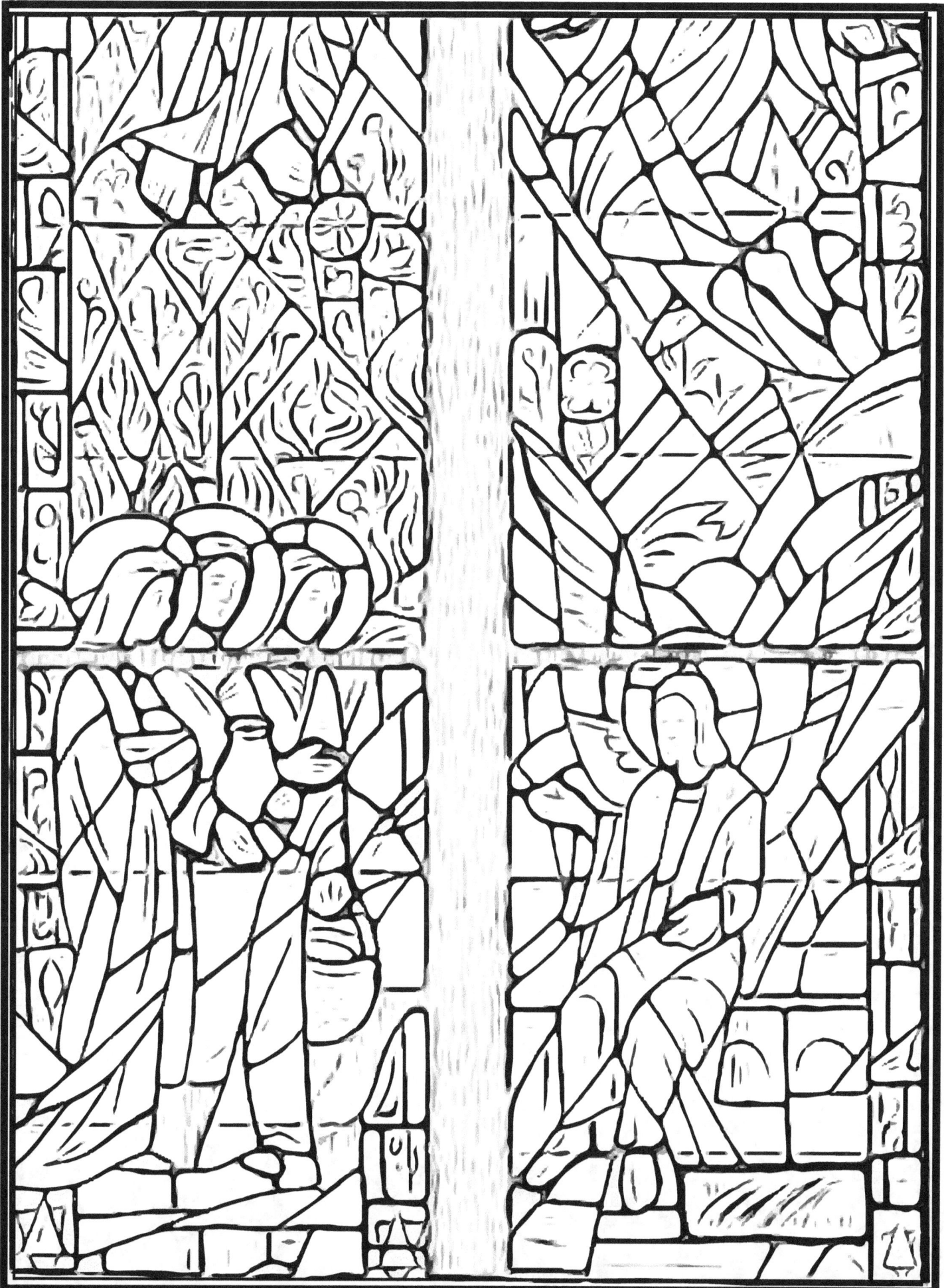

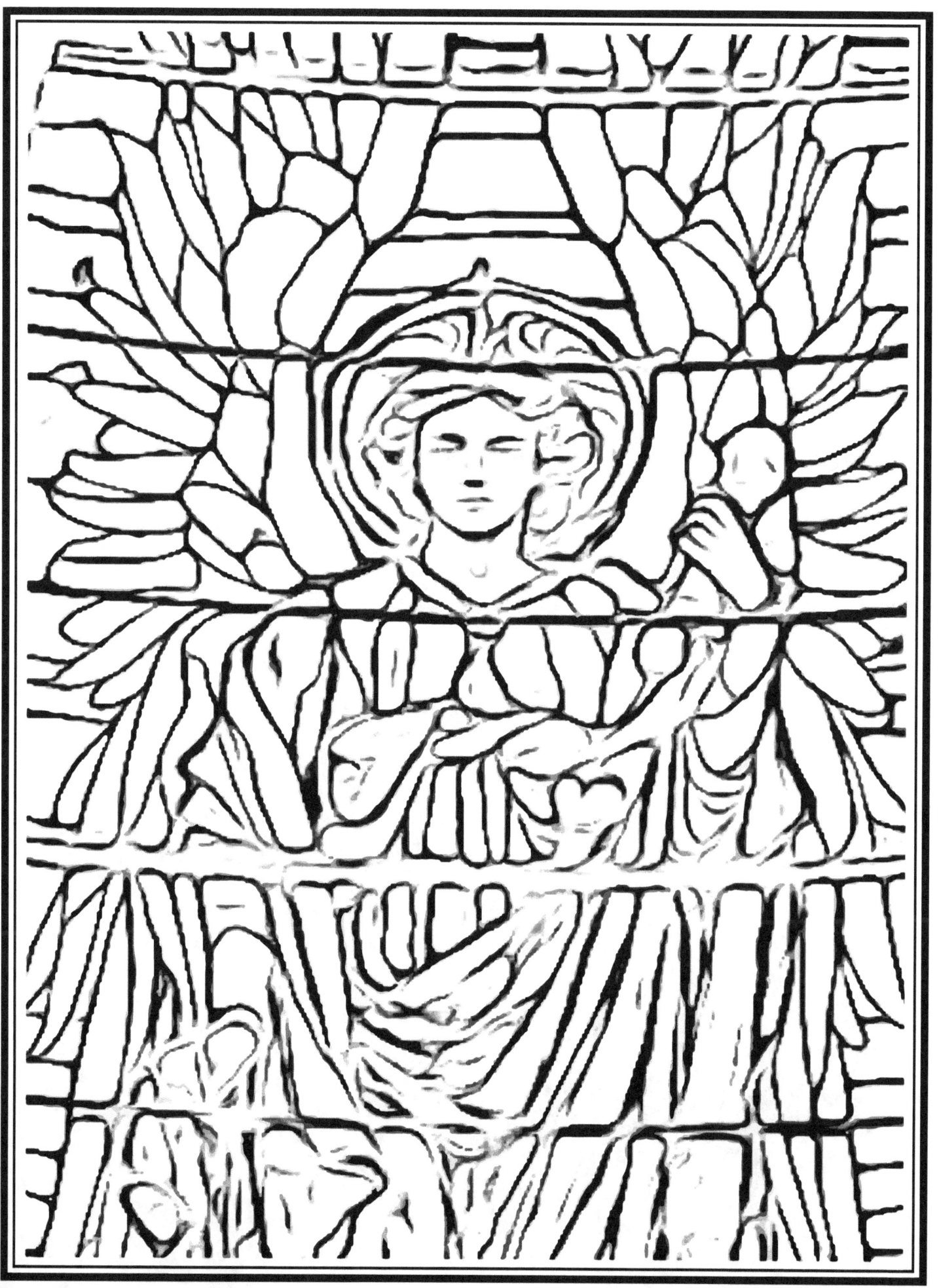

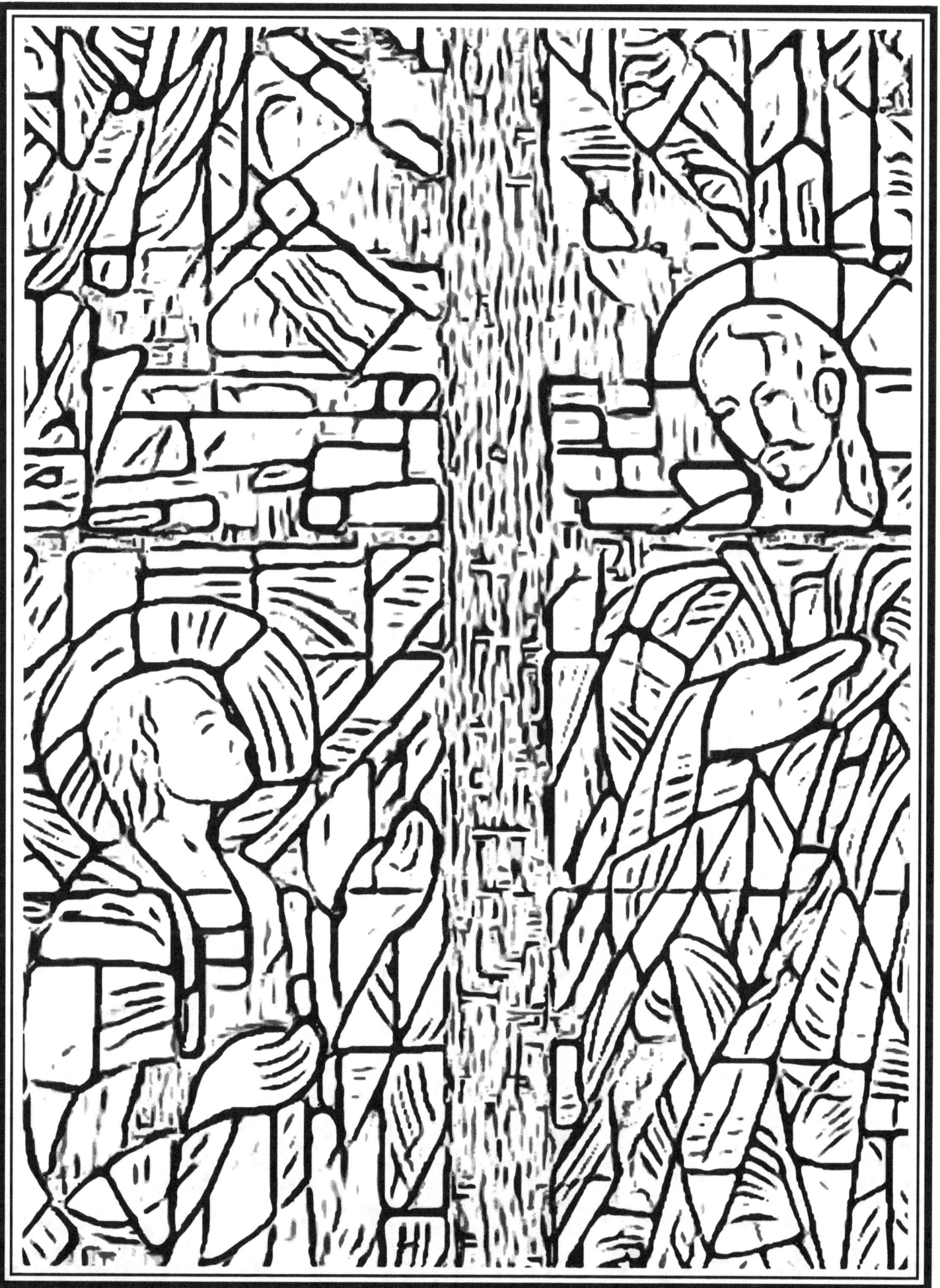

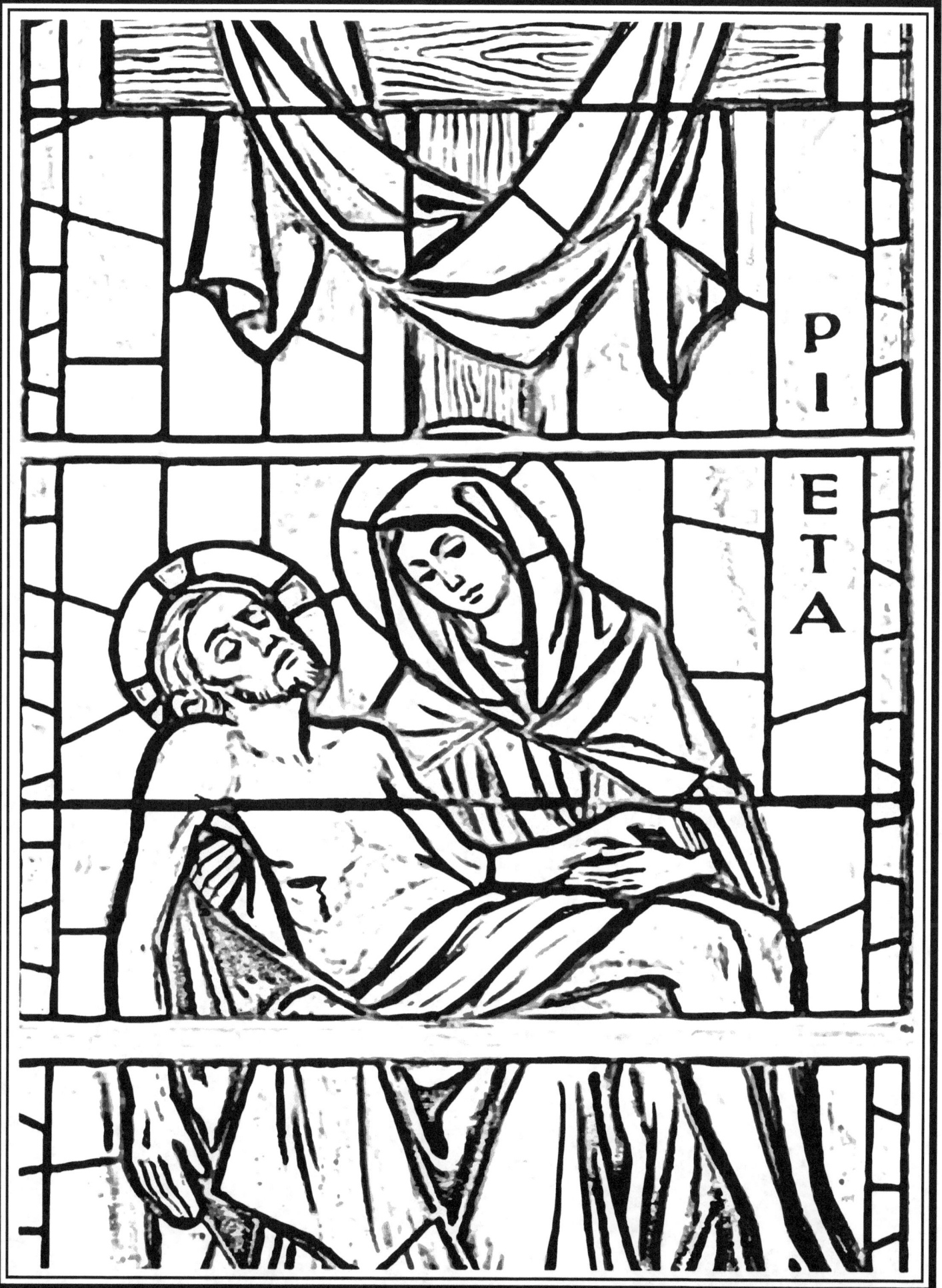

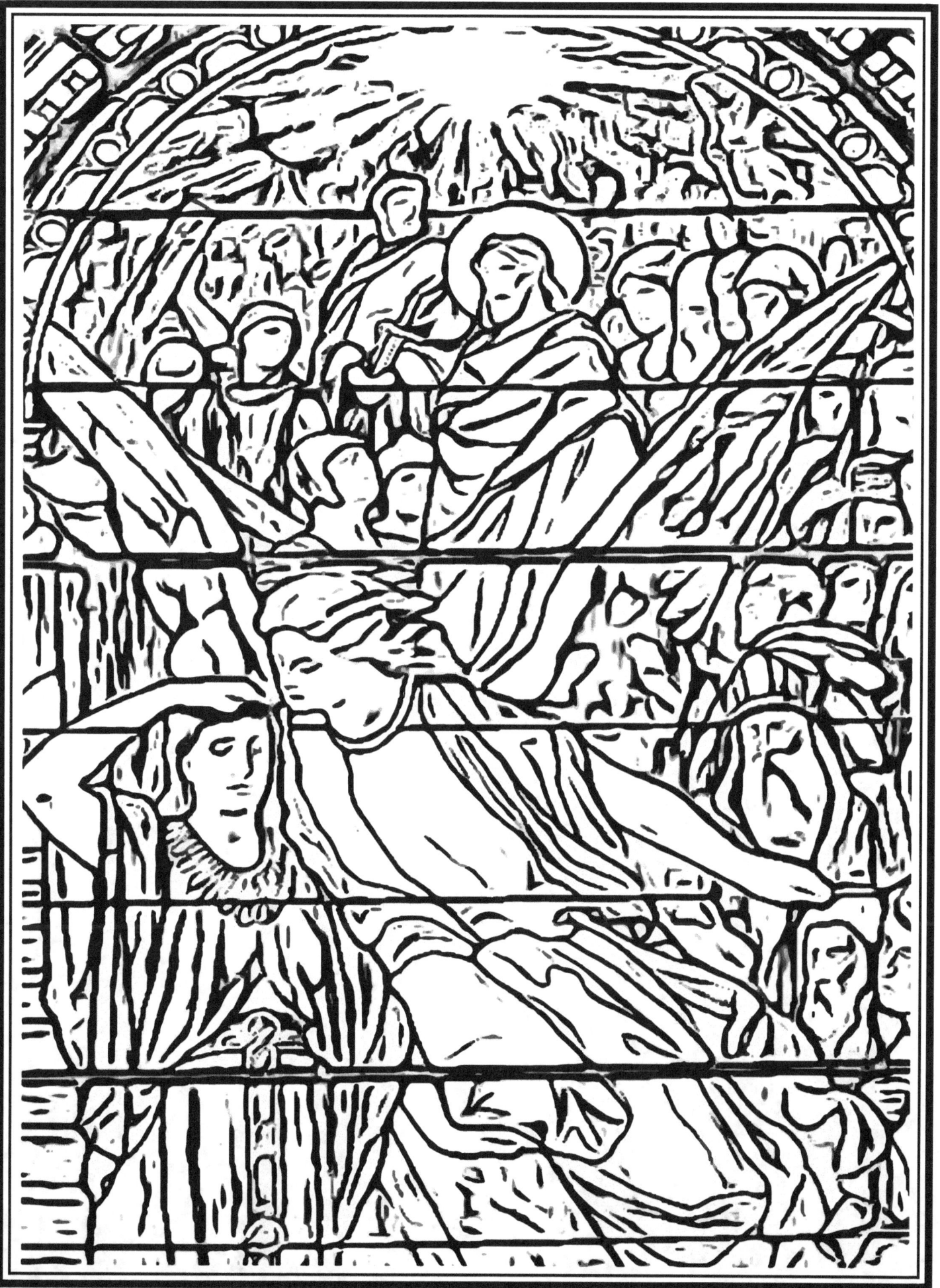

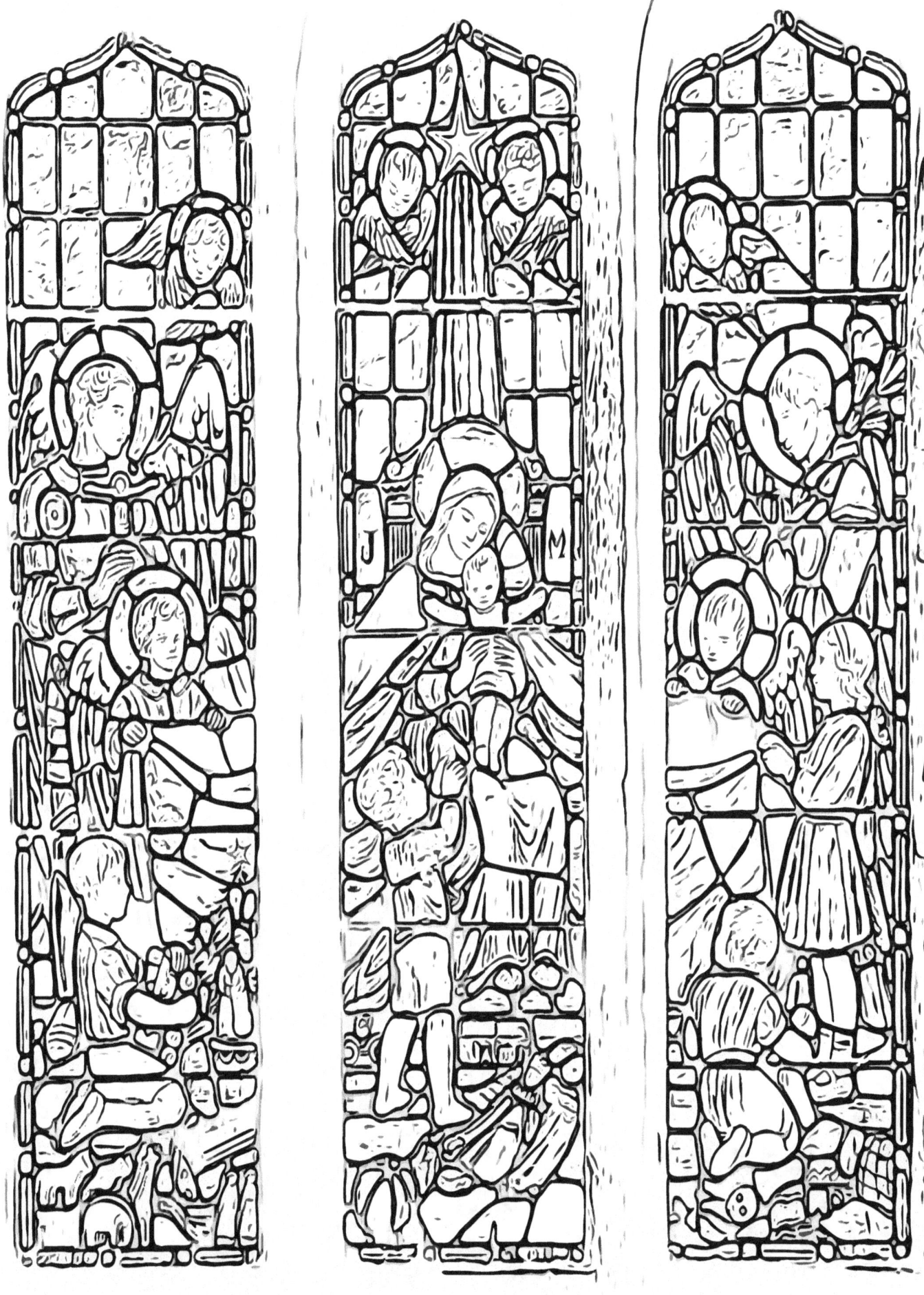

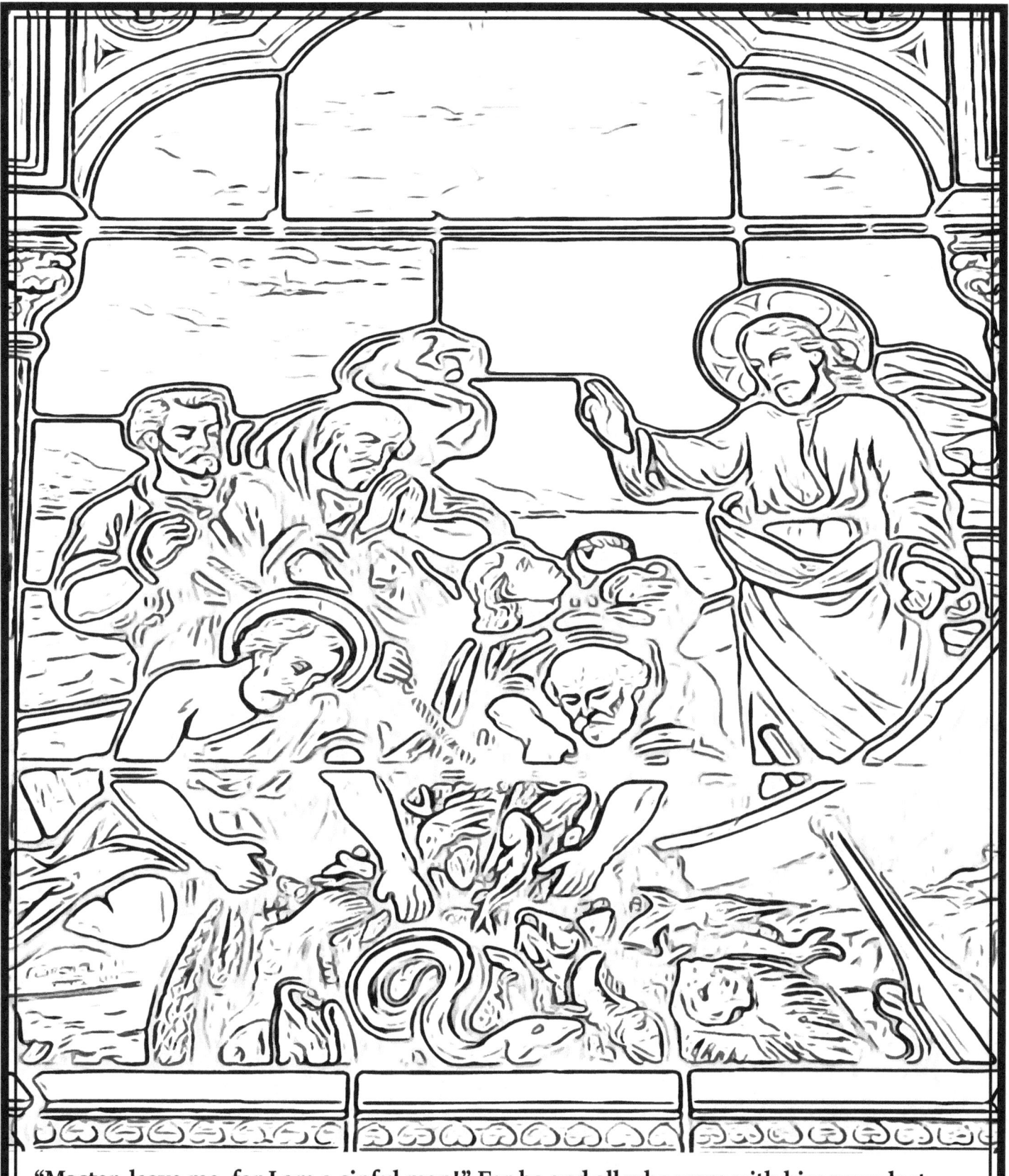

"Master, leave me, for I am a sinful man!" For he and all who were with him were lost in amazement at the haul of fish which they had made; and so, too, were James and John, Zebedee's sons, who were Simon's partners. "Do not be afraid," Jesus said to Simon; "from today you will catch people." And, when they had brought their boats to shore, they left everything, and followed him. Luke 5:8-11 OEB

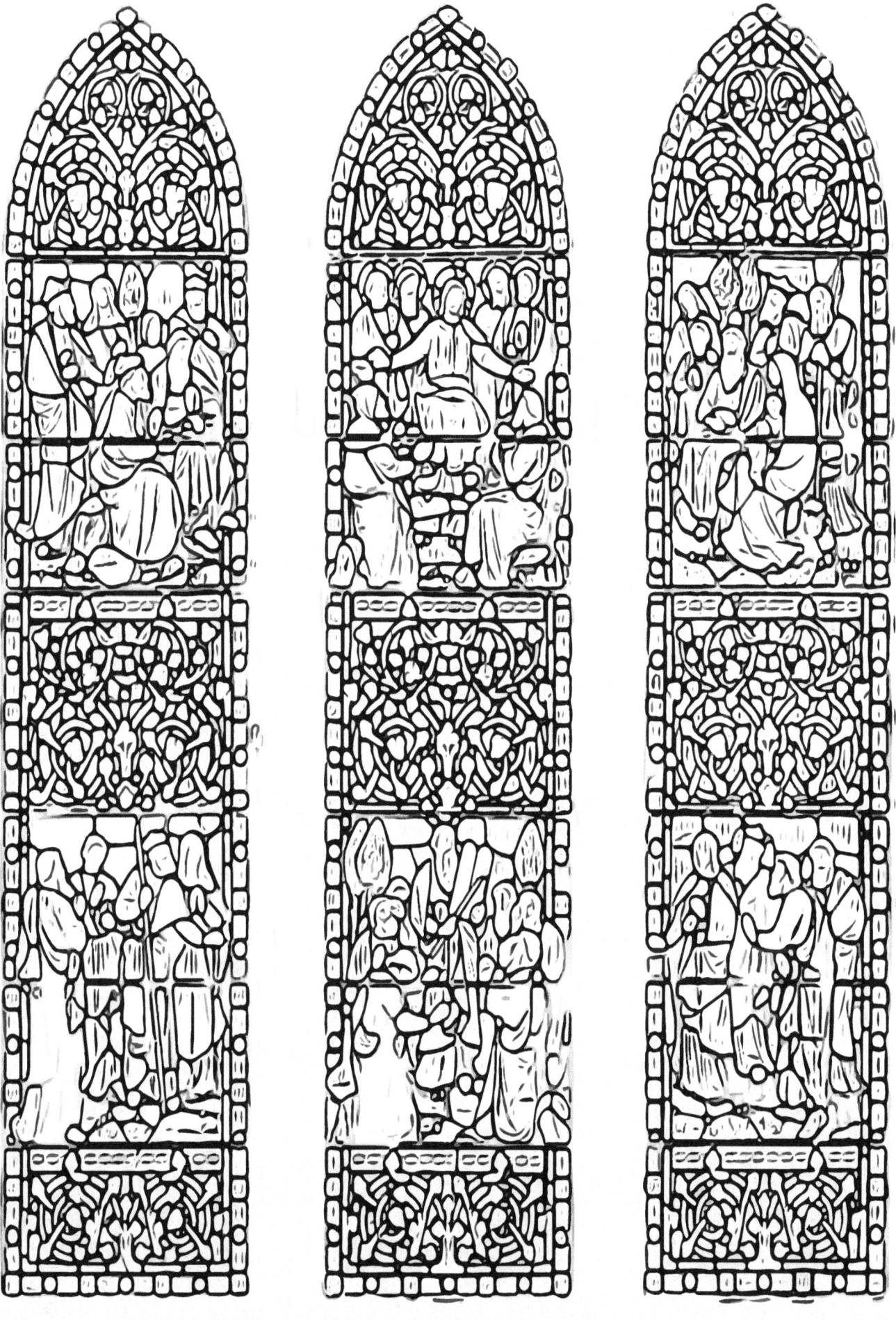

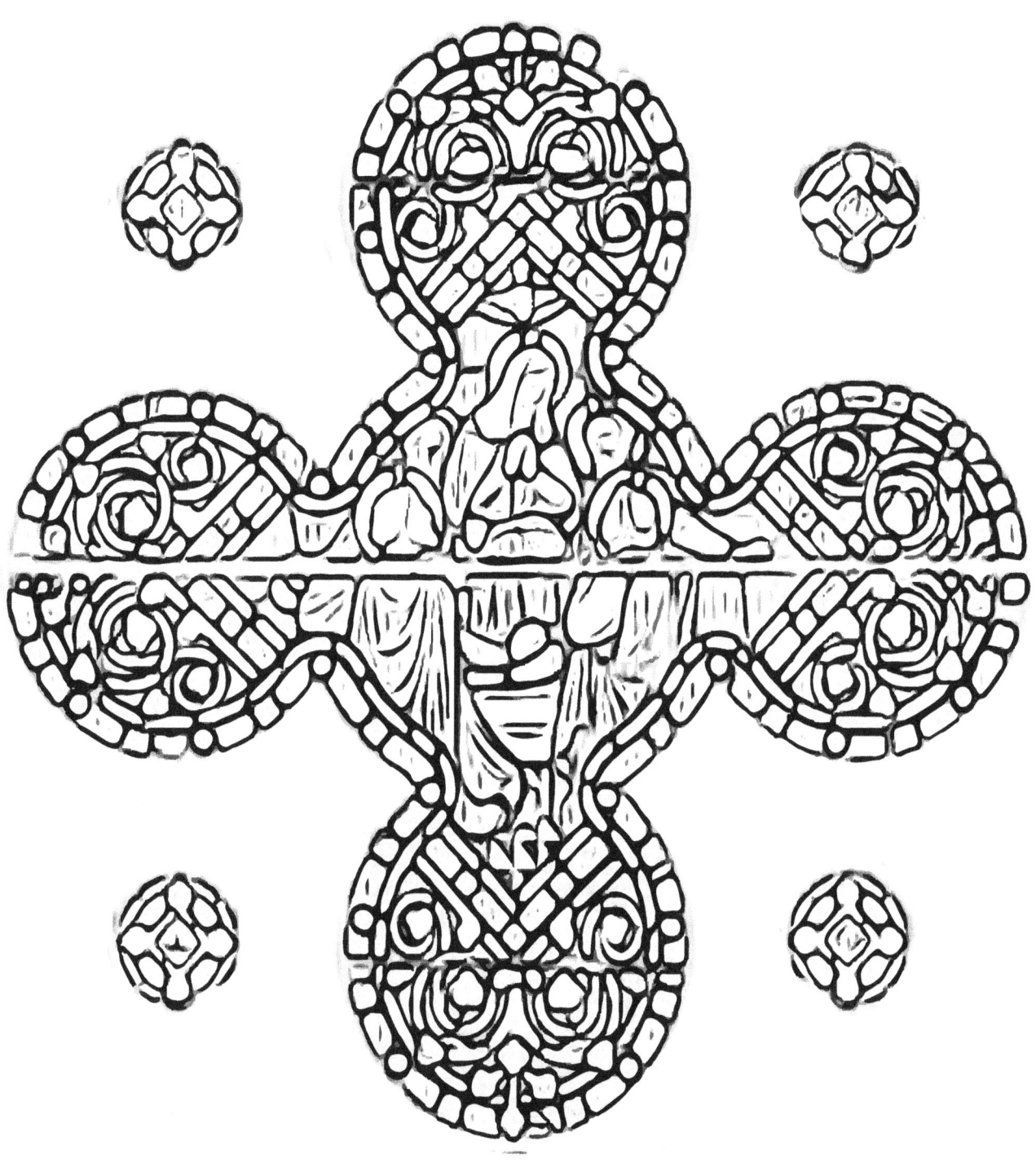

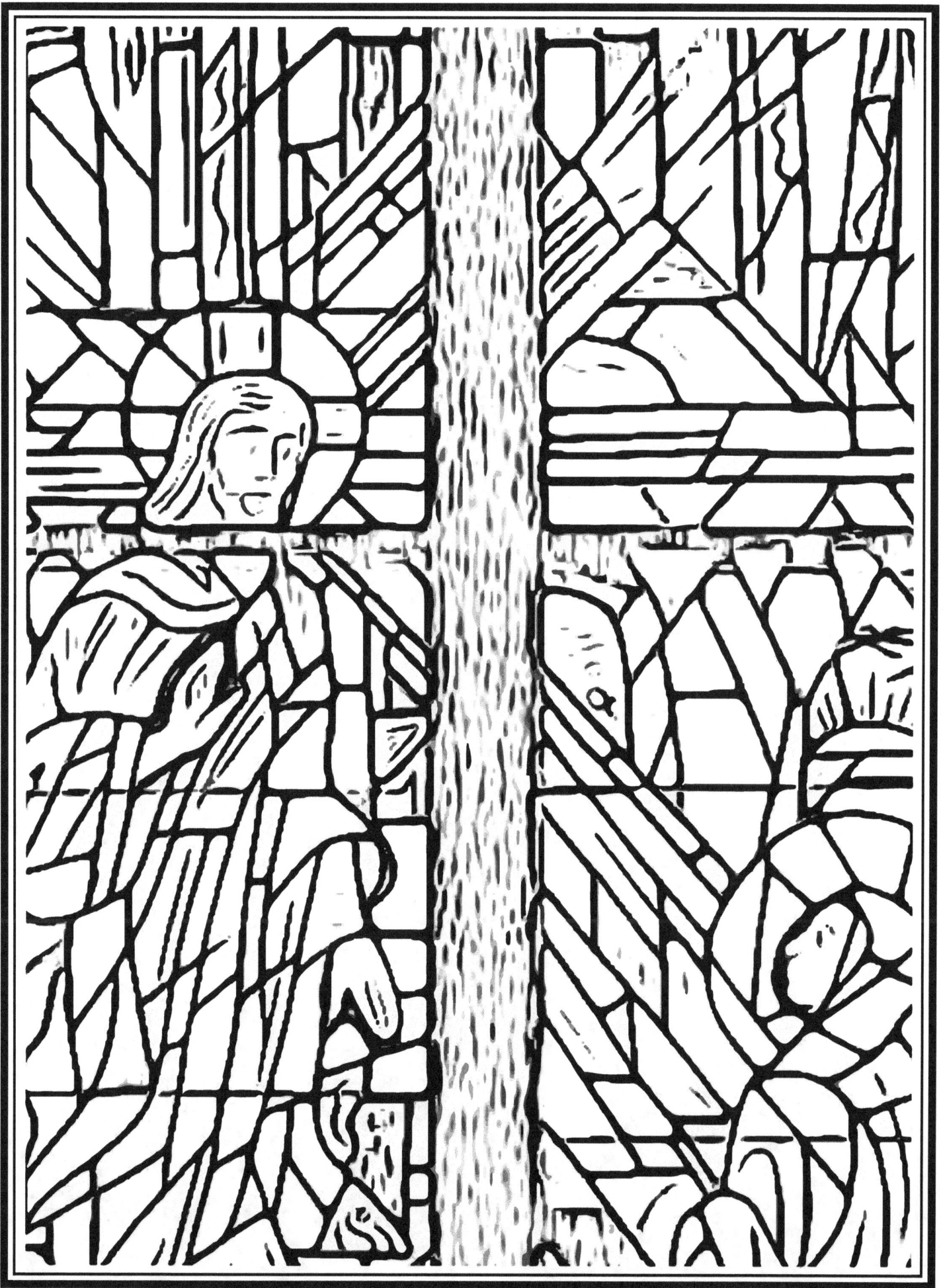

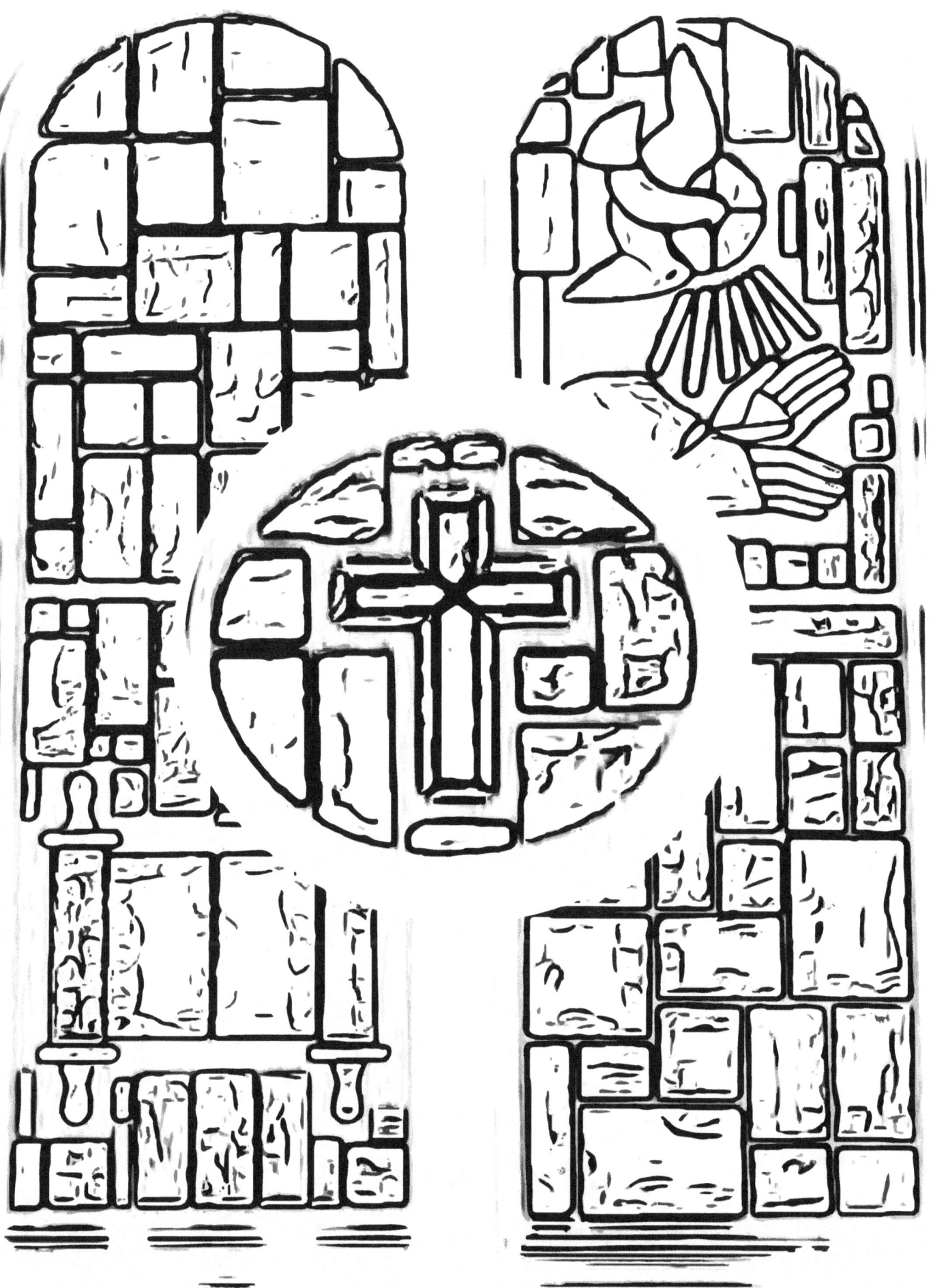

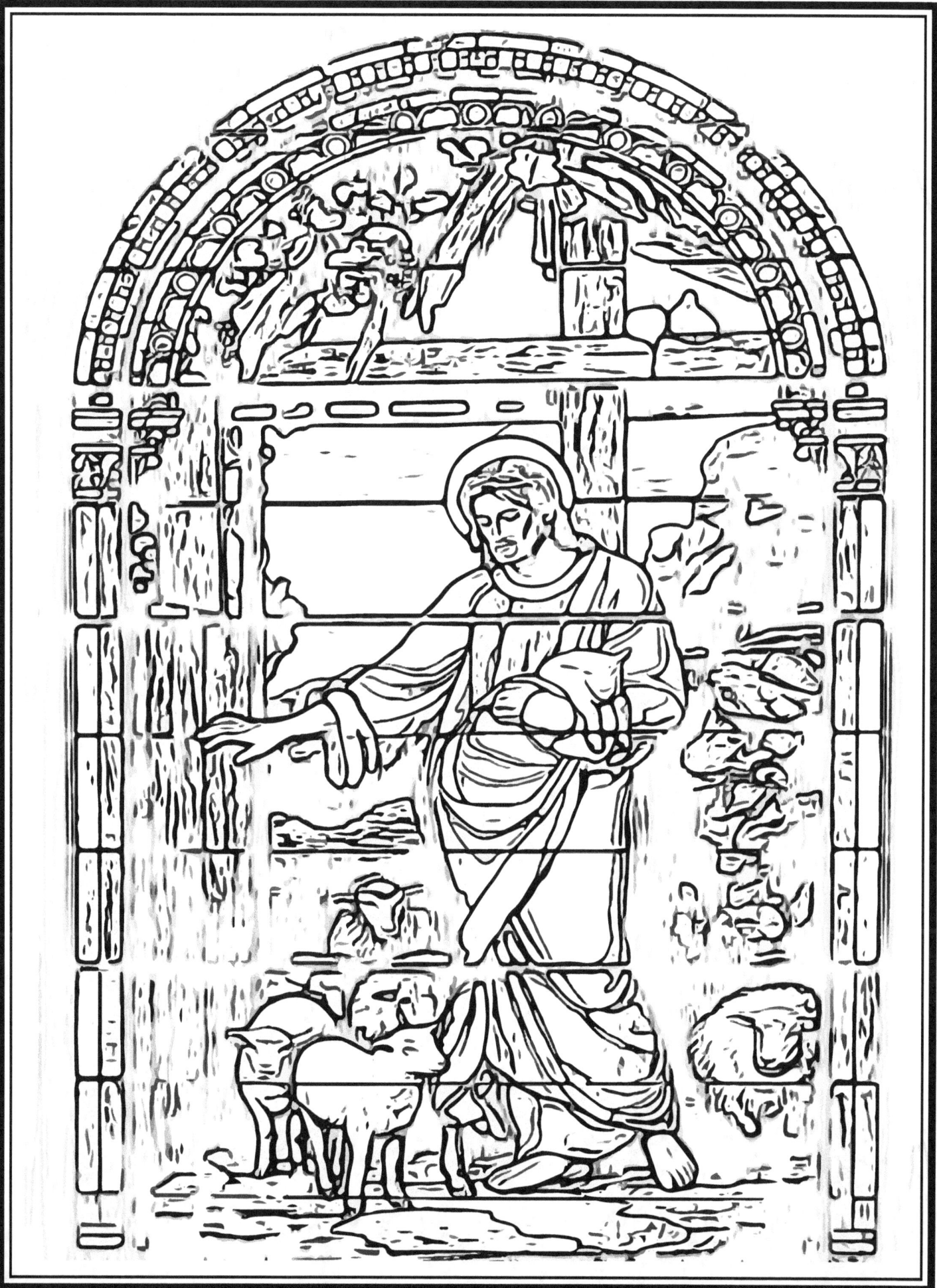

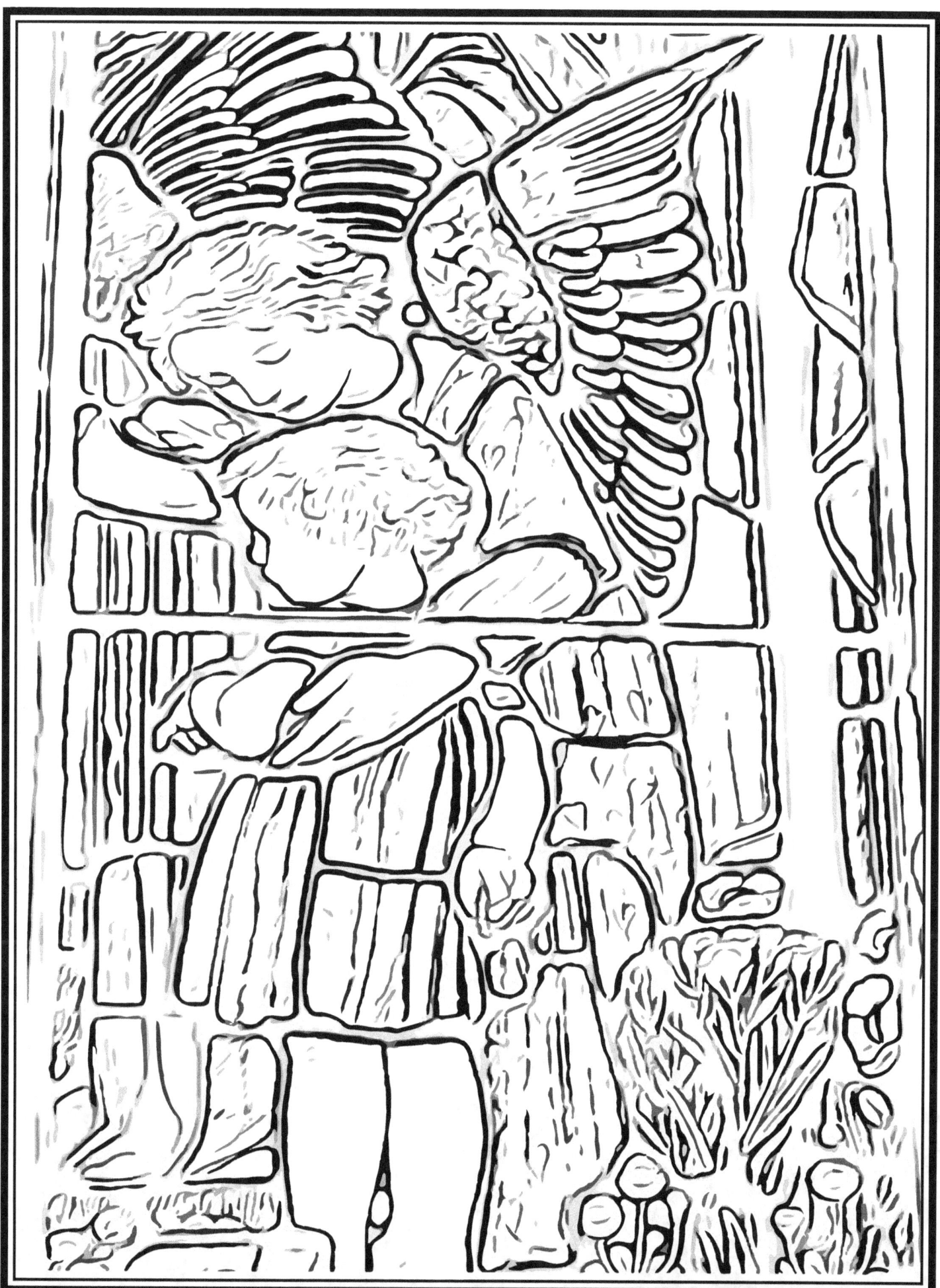

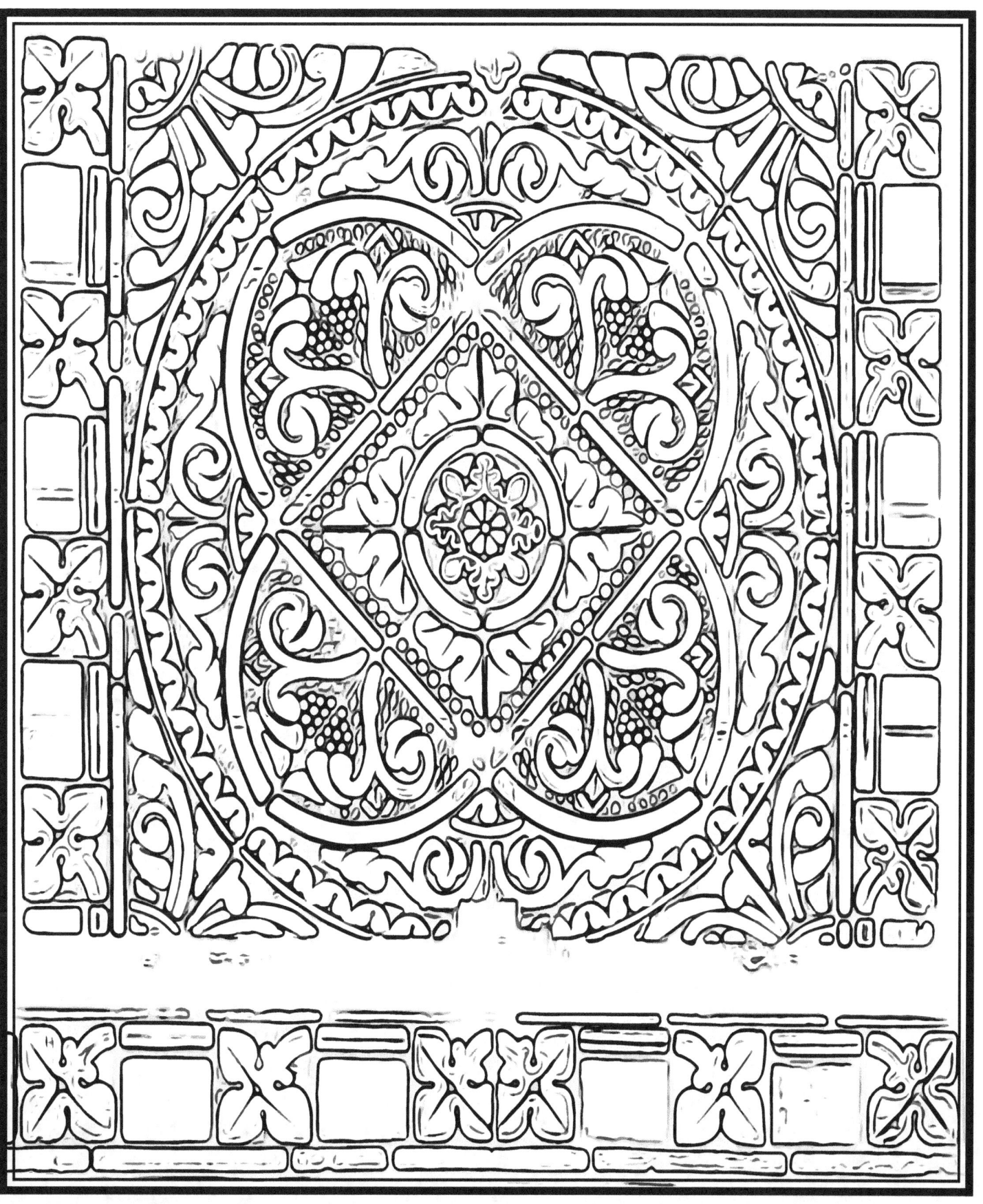

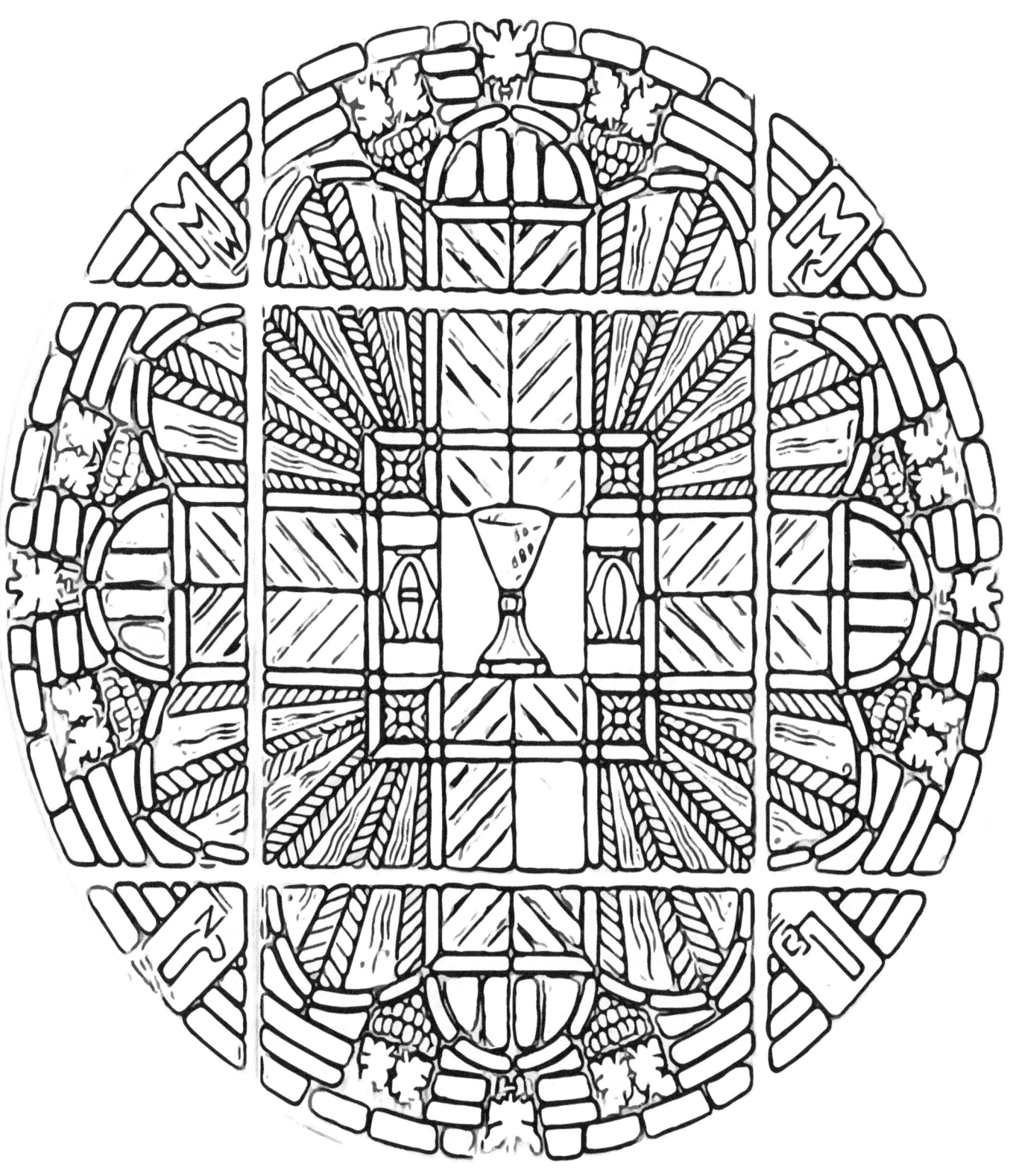

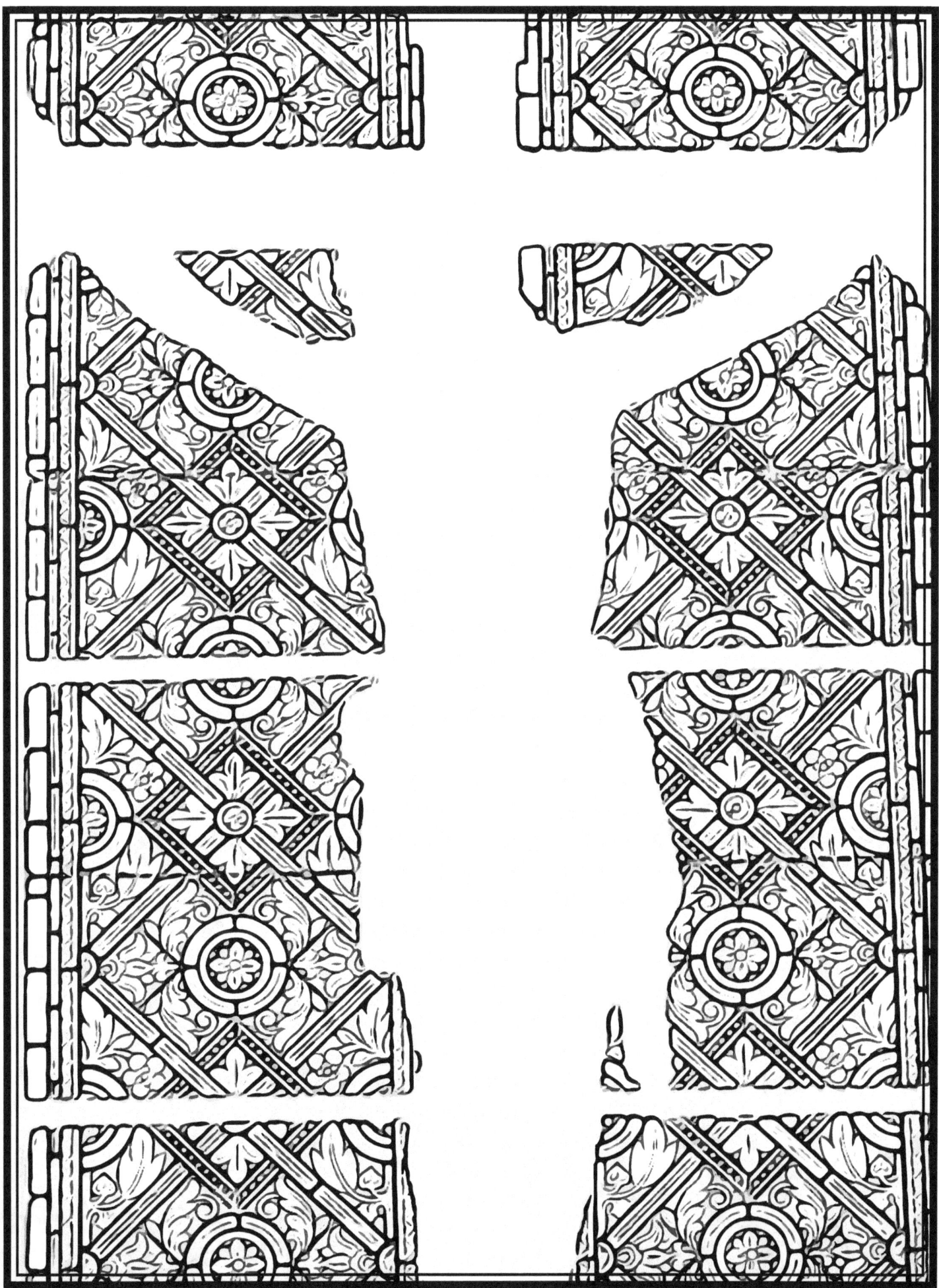

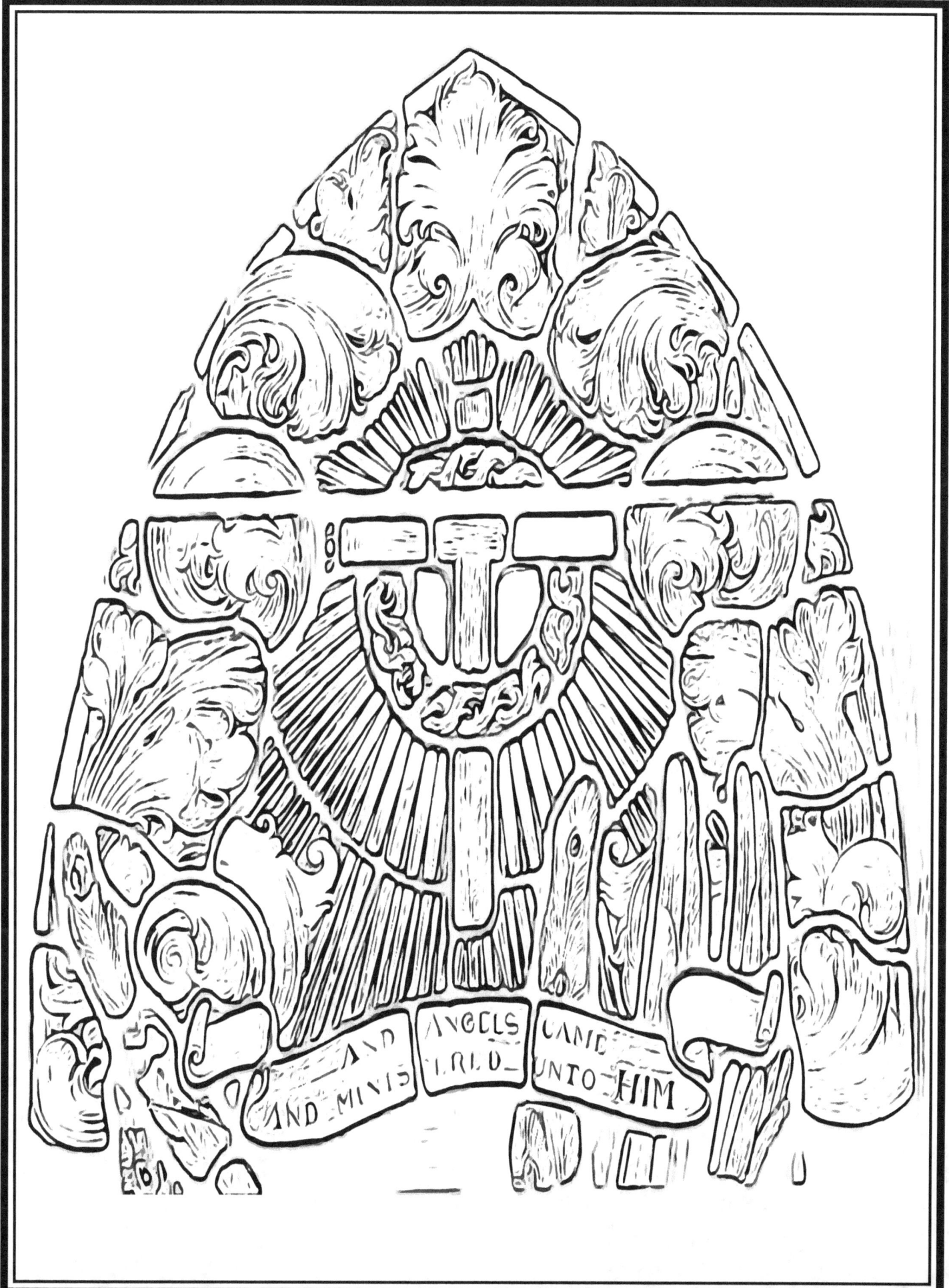

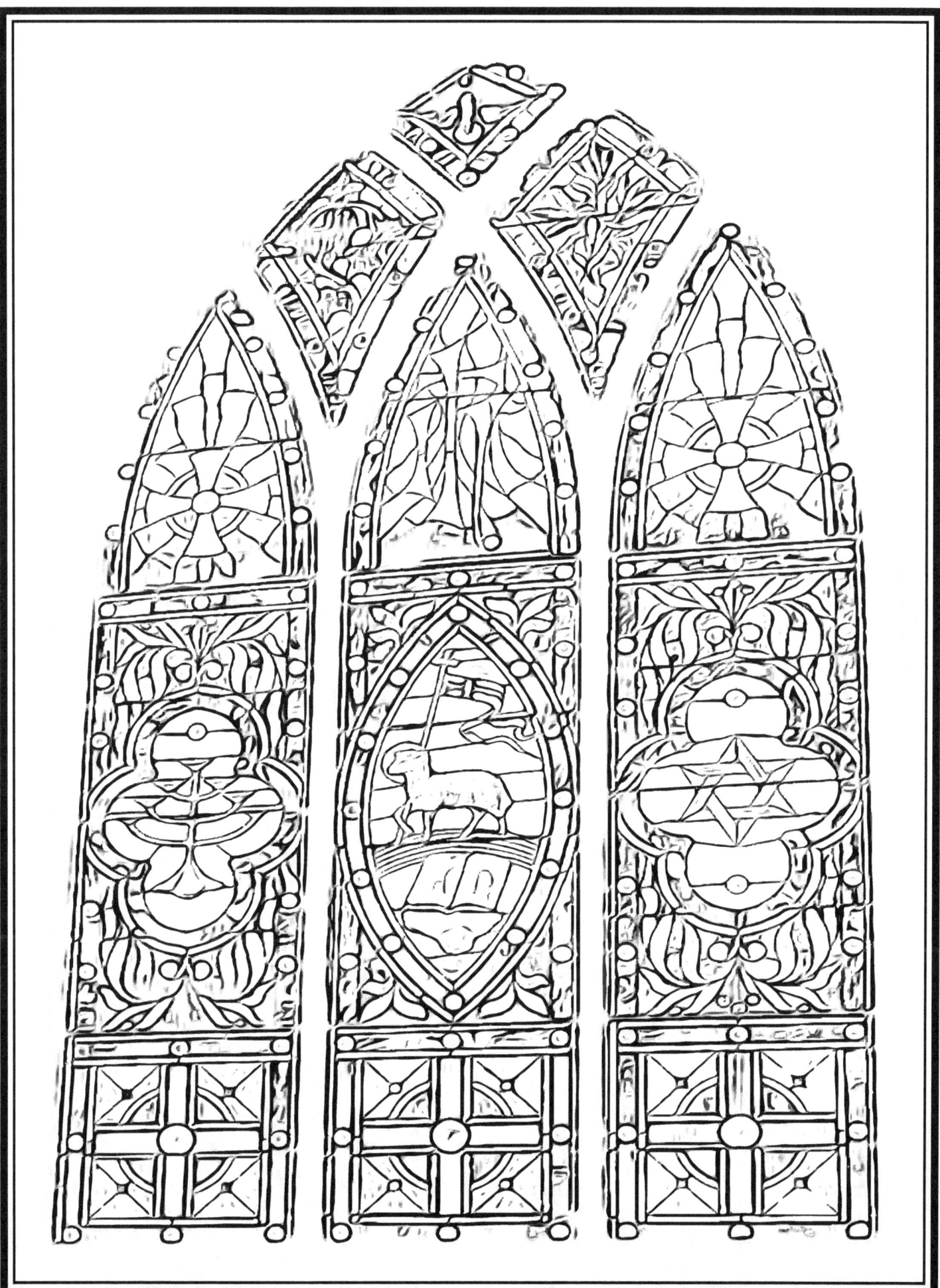

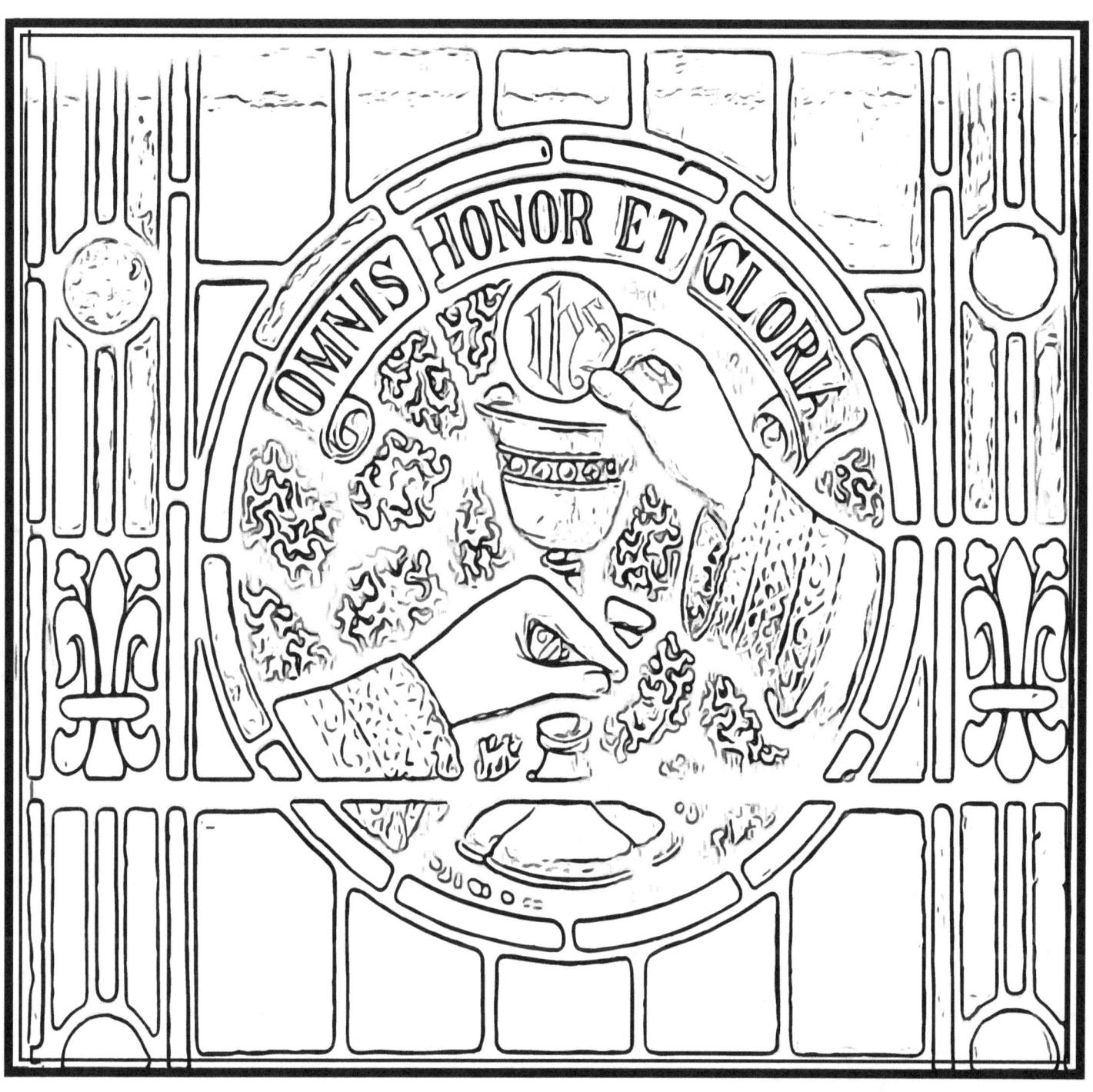

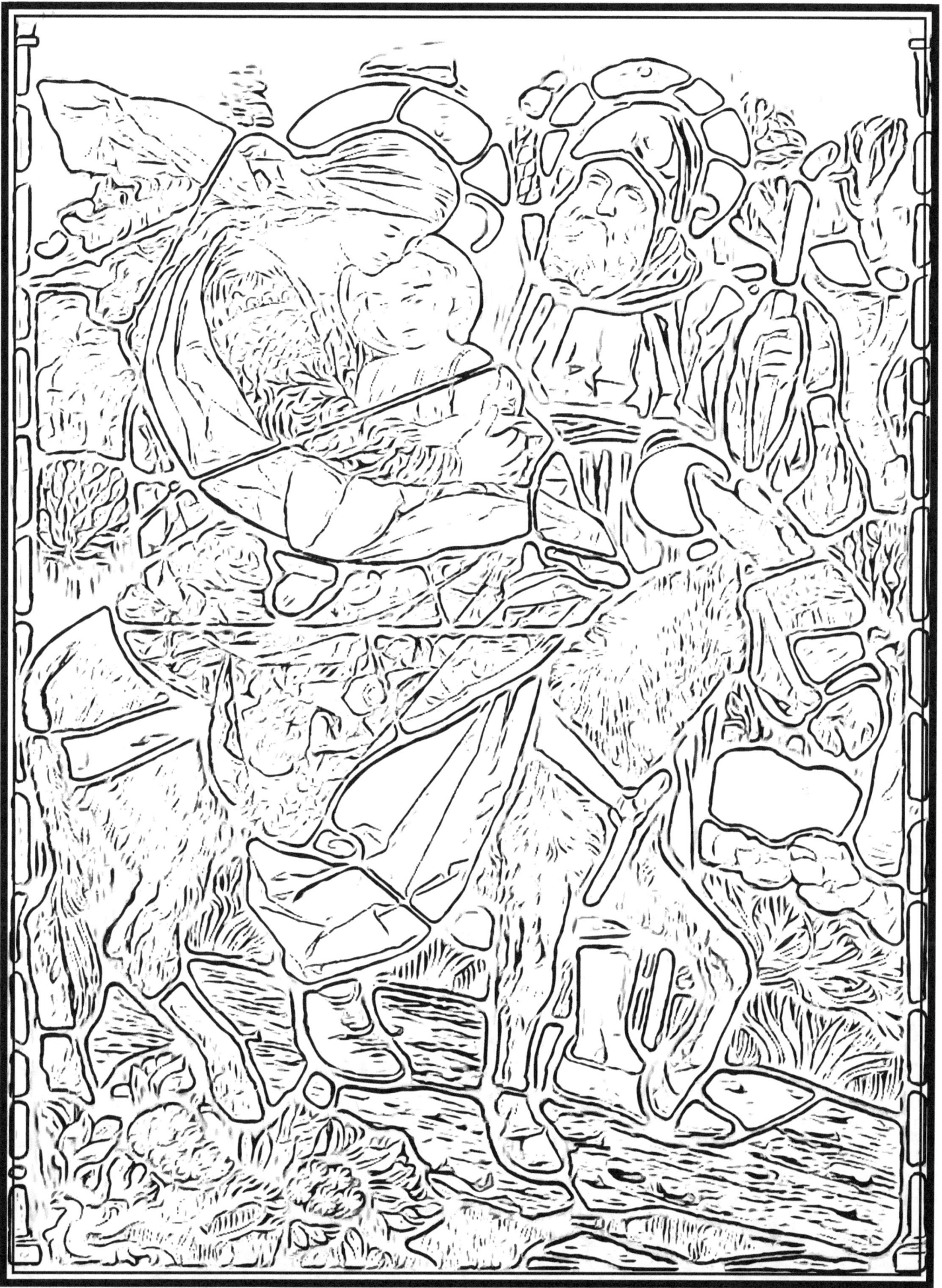

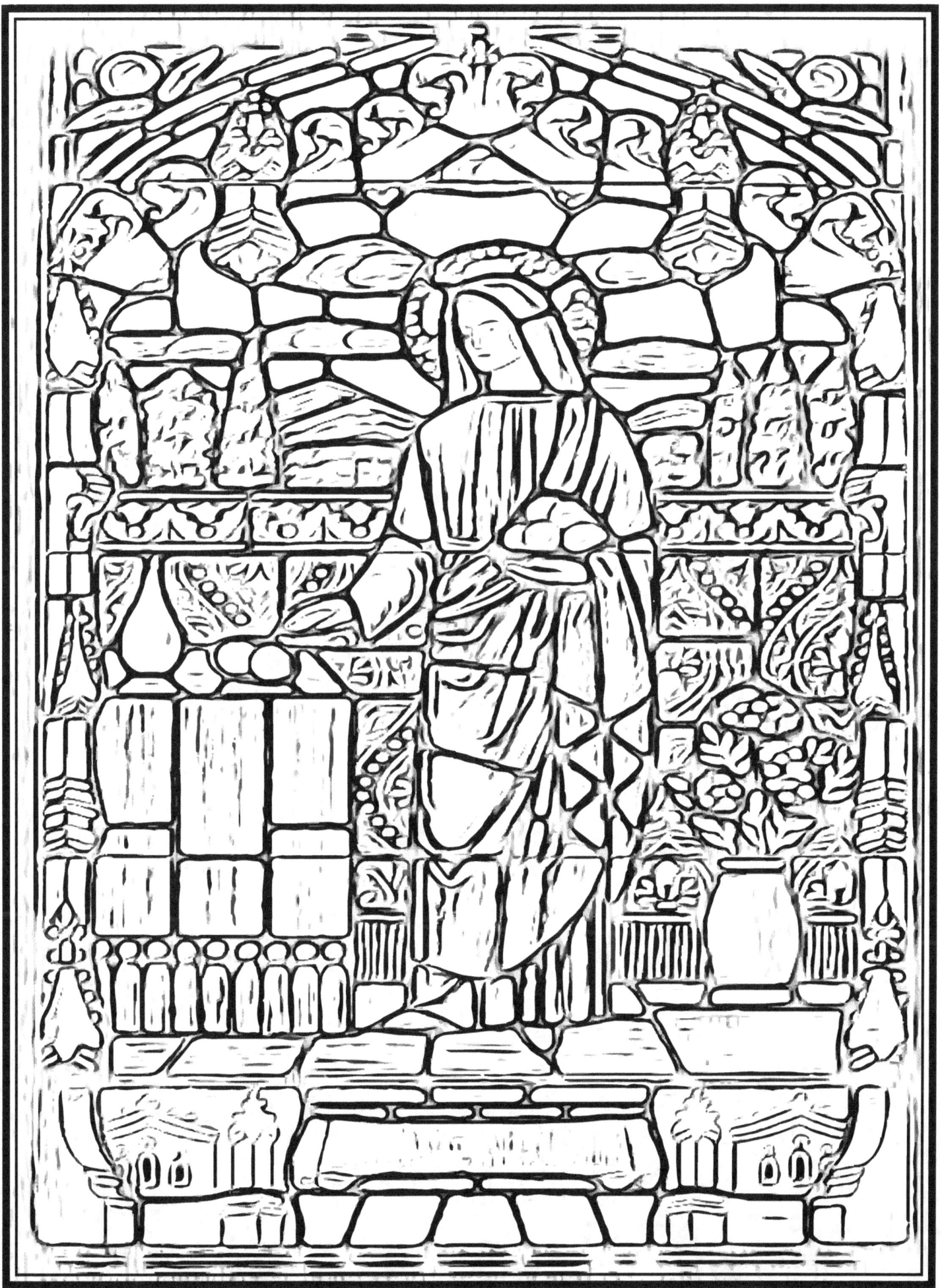

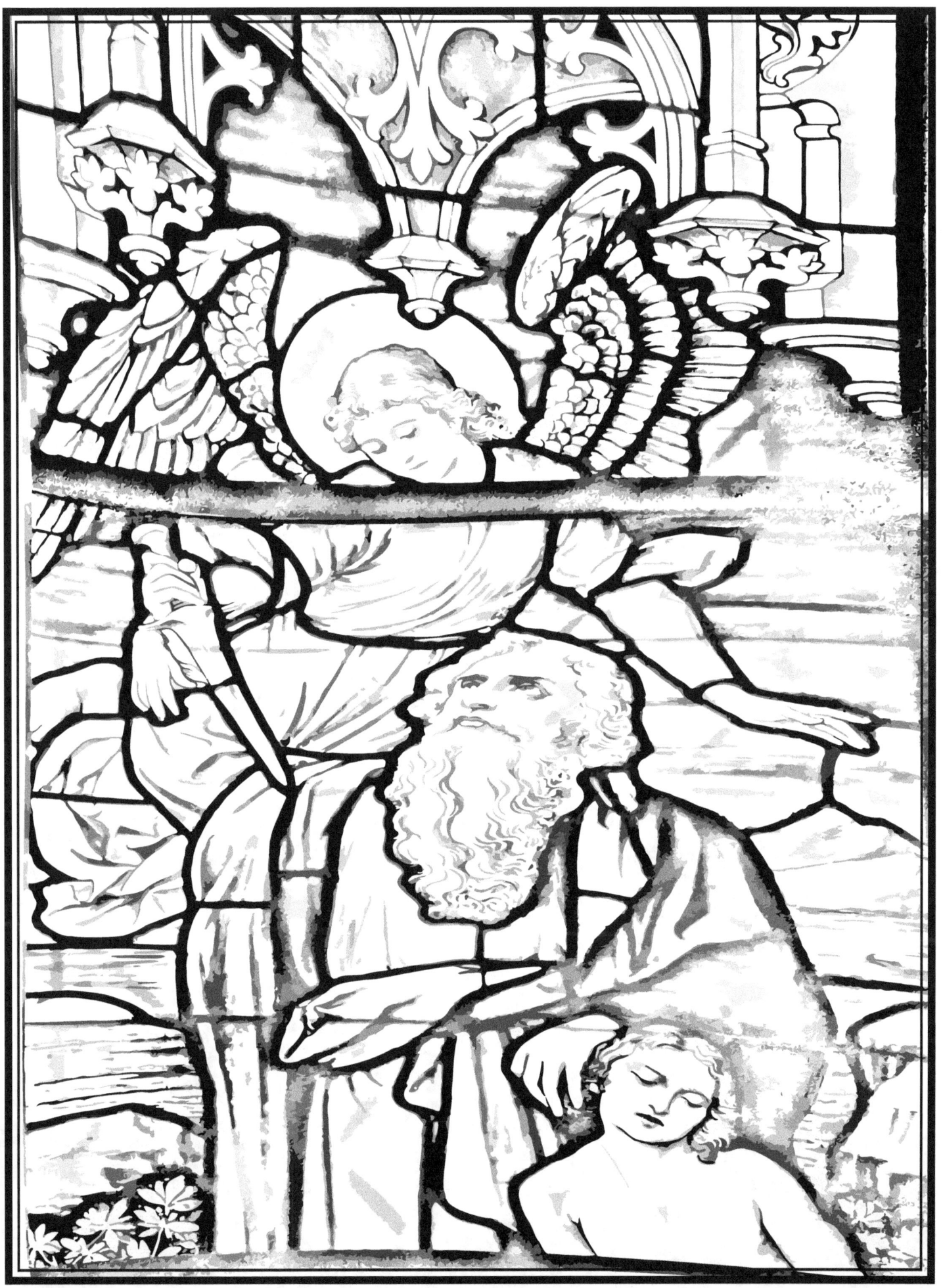

The Storms

The Winds

The Waves

They still know His Name!

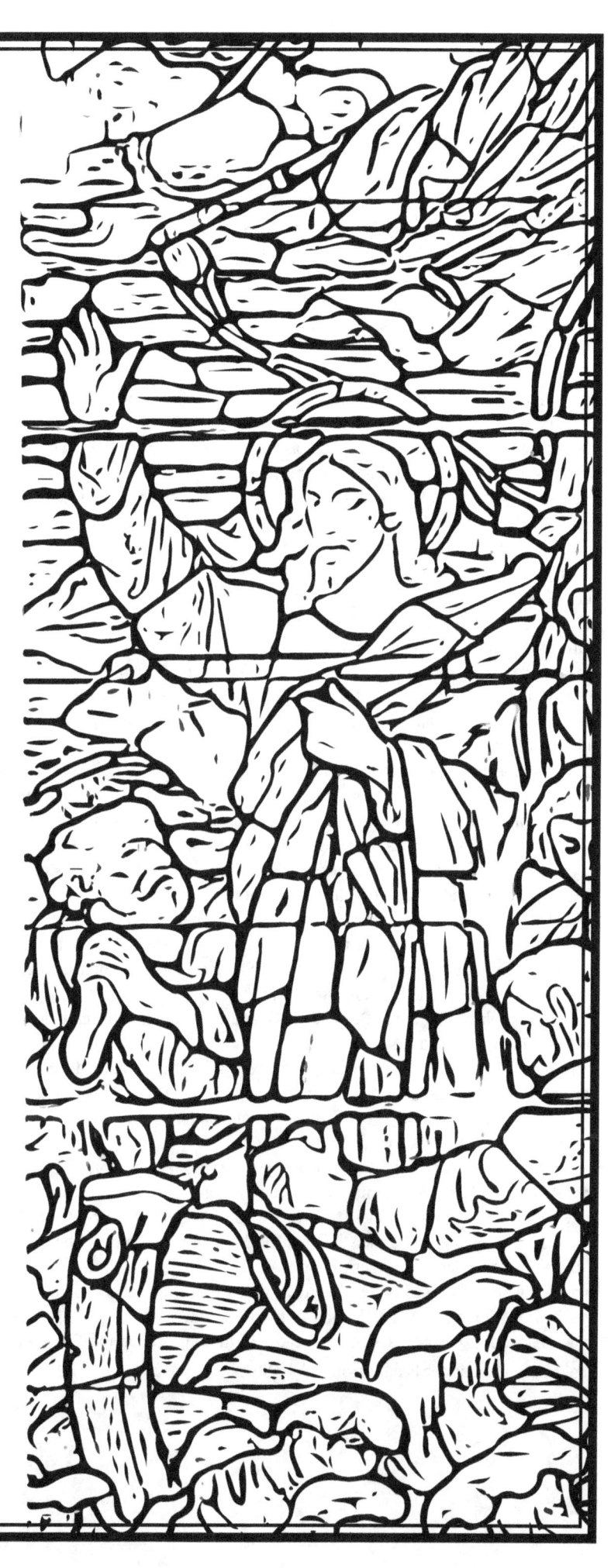

Photo and Image Credits

Additional FREE Coloring Pages

These images come to you from around the world, some from churches in my local area, some from across the U.S., and some from churches in Europe and Asia. If you enjoyed this selection of church windows, please help me and other adult Christians by posting feedback on Amazon.com or your favorite online bookstore. If you do, drop me an email at GreatColoradoBooks@gmail.com, and I will be glad to send you five additional coloring pages for free that you can print at home.

If you have any suggestions for improvement or have ideas for other coloring book designs that would honor the Christian faith, please contact me as well. Again, my email address is GreatColoradoBooks@gmail.com.

For more information on this book, go to www.StainedNoMore.com.

God bless you, and I look forward to hearing from you soon!